I Remember Nothing

I Remember Nothing

AND OTHER REFLECTIONS

Nora Ephron

RANDOM HOUSE
LARGE PRINT

Cover design by Abby Weintraub

Some of the pieces in this collection have previously appeared in the
following: "Christmas Dinner," "I Just Want to Say: Teflon" as
"Farewell to Teflon," "I Just Want to Say: The Egg-White Omelette"
as "The Informational Cascade and the Egg-White Omelette,"
"I Just Want to Say: The World Is Not Flat" as "And by the Way, the
World Is Not Flat," "Twenty-Five Things People Have a Shocking
Capacity to Be Surprised by Over and Over Again" in The
Huffington Post; "Addicted to L-U-V," "Going to the Movies" as
"The Last Picture Show," "I Just Want to Say: Chicken Soup" as
"The Chicken Soup Chronicles," "I Just Want to Say: No, I Do Not
Want Another Bottle of Pellegrino" as "What to Expect When You're
Expecting Dinner," "The Six Stages of E-Mail," and "Who Are
You?" in The New York Times; "My Life as an Heiress" in The New
Yorker; and "The Legend" in Vogue.

The Library of Congress has established a Cataloging-in-Publication
record for this title.

ISBN: 978-0-7393-7804-5

www.randomhouse.com/largeprint

FIRST LARGE PRINT EDITION

Printed in the United States of America

10 9 8 7 6 5 4 3 2 1

This Large Print edition published in accord with
the standards of the N.A.V.H.

For Richard and Mona

Contents

Contents

Contents

I Remember Nothing

I Remember Nothing

I have been forgetting things for years—at least since I was in my thirties. I know this because I wrote something about it at the time. I have proof. Of course, I can't remember exactly where I wrote about it, or when, but I could probably hunt it up if I had to.

In my early days of forgetting things, words would slip away, and names. I did what you normally do when this happens: I scrolled through a mental dictionary, trying to figure out what letter the word began with, and how many syllables were involved. Eventually the lost thing would float back into my head, recaptured. I never took such lapses as harbingers of doom, or old age, or actual senescence. I always knew that whatever I'd forgotten was going to come back to me sooner or later. Once I went to a store to buy a book about Alzheimer's disease and forgot the name of it. I thought it was funny. And it was, at the time.

Here's a thing I've never been able to remember: the title of that movie with Jeremy Irons. The one about Claus von Bülow. You know the one. All I ever succeeded in remembering was that it was three words long, and the middle word was "of." For many years, this did not bother me at all, because no one I knew could ever think of the title either. One night, eight of us were at the theater together, and not one of us could retrieve it. Finally, at intermission, someone went out to the street and Googled it; we were all informed of the title and we all vowed to remember it forever. For all I know, the other seven did. I, on the other hand, am back to remembering that it's three words long with an "of" in the middle.

By the way, when we finally learned the title that night, we all agreed it was a bad title. No wonder we didn't remember it.

I am going to Google for the name of that movie. Be right back. . . .

It's **Reversal of Fortune.**

I Remember Nothing

How is one to remember that title? It has nothing to do with anything.

But here's the point: I have been forgetting things for years, but now I forget in a new way. I used to believe I could eventually retrieve whatever was lost and then commit it to memory. Now I know I can't possibly. Whatever's gone is hopelessly gone. And what's new doesn't stick.

The other night I met a man who informed me that he had a neurological disorder and couldn't remember the faces of people he'd met. He said that sometimes he looked at himself in a mirror and had no idea whom he was looking at. I don't mean to minimize this man's ailment, which I'm sure is a bona fide syndrome with a long name that's capitalized, but all I could think was, Welcome to my world. A couple of years ago, the actor Ryan O'Neal confessed that he'd recently failed to recognize his own daughter, Tatum, at a funeral and had accidentally made a pass at her. Everyone was judgmental about this, but not me. A month earlier, I'd found myself in a mall in Las Vegas when I saw a very pleasant-looking woman coming toward me, smiling, her arms outstretched, and I thought, Who is this woman? Where do I know her from? Then she spoke and I realized it was my sister Amy.

You might think, Well, how was she to know her sister would be in Las Vegas? I'm sorry to report that not only did I know, but she was the person I was meeting in the mall.

All this makes me feel sad, and wistful, but mostly it makes me feel old. I have many symptoms of old age, aside from the physical. I occasionally repeat myself. I use the expression, "When I was young." Often I don't get the joke, although I pretend that I do. If I go see a play or a movie for a second time, it's as if I didn't see it at all the first time, even if the first time was just recently. I have no idea who anyone in **People** magazine is.

I used to think my problem was that my disk was full; now I'm forced to conclude that the opposite is true: it's becoming empty.

I have not yet reached the nadir of old age, the Land of Anecdote, but I'm approaching it.

I know, I know, I should have kept a journal. I should have saved the love letters. I should have taken a storage room somewhere in Long Island City for all the papers I thought I'd never need to look at again.

But I didn't.

And sometimes I'm forced to conclude that I remember nothing.

For example: I met Eleanor Roosevelt. It was June 1961, and I was on my way to a political internship at the Kennedy White House. All the Wellesley/Vassar interns drove to Hyde Park to meet the former first lady. I was dying to meet her. I'd grown up with a photograph in our den of her standing with my parents backstage at a play they'd written. My mother was wearing a corsage and Eleanor wore pearls. It was a photograph I always thought of as iconic, if I'm using the word correctly, which, if I am, it will be for the first time. We were among the thousands of Americans (mostly Jews) who had dens, and, in their dens, photos of Eleanor Roosevelt. I idolized the woman. I couldn't believe I was going to be in the same room with her. So what was she like that day in Hyde Park, you may wonder. I HAVE NO IDEA. I can't remember what she said or what she wore; I can barely summon up a mental picture of the room where we met her, although I have a very vague memory of drapes. But here's what I do remember: I got lost on the way. And ever since, every time I've been on the Taconic State Parkway, I'm reminded that I got lost there on the way to meet Eleanor Roosevelt. But I don't remember a thing about Eleanor Roosevelt herself.

In 1964 the Beatles came to New York for the first time. I was a newspaper reporter and I was sent to the airport to cover their arrival. It was a Friday. I spent the weekend following them around. Sunday night they appeared on **The Ed Sullivan Show.** You could make an argument that the sixties began that night, on **The Ed Sullivan Show.** It was a historic night. I was there. I stood in the back of the Ed Sullivan Theater and watched. I remember how amazingly obnoxious the fans were—the teenage girls who screamed and yelled and behaved like idiots. But how were the Beatles, you may ask. Well, you are asking the wrong person. I could barely hear them.

I marched on Washington to protest the war in Vietnam. This was in 1967, and it was the most significant event of the antiwar movement. Thousands and thousands of people were there. I went with a lawyer I was dating. We spent most of the day in a hotel room having sex. I am not proud of this, but I mention it because it explains why I honestly cannot remember anything about the protest, including whether I ever even got to the Pentagon. I don't think I did. I don't think I've ever been to the Pentagon. But I wouldn't bet a nickel on it one way or the other.

Norman Mailer wrote an entire book about this march, called **The Armies of the Night**. It was 288 pages long. It won the Pulitzer Prize. And I can barely write two paragraphs about it. If you knew Norman Mailer and me and were asked to guess which of us cared more about sex, you would, of course, pick Norman Mailer. How wrong you would be.

Here are some people I met that I remember nothing about:

Justice Hugo Black
Ethel Merman
Jimmy Stewart
Alger Hiss
Senator Hubert Humphrey
Cary Grant
Benny Goodman
Peter Ustinov
Harry Kurnitz
George Abbott
Dorothy Parker

I went to the Bobby Riggs–Billie Jean King tennis match and couldn't really see anything from where I was sitting.

I went to stand in front of the White House the night Nixon resigned and here's what I have to tell you about it: my wallet was stolen.

I went to many legendary rock concerts and spent them wondering when they would end and where we would eat afterward and whether the restaurant would still be open and what I would order.

I went to at least one hundred Knicks games and I remember only the night that Reggie Miller scored eight points in the last nine seconds.

I went to cover the war in Israel in 1973 but my therapist absolutely forbid me to go to the front.

I was not at Woodstock, but I might as well have been because I wouldn't remember it anyway.

On some level, my life has been wasted on me. After all, if I can't remember it, who can?

The past is slipping away and the present is a constant affront. I can't possibly keep up. When I was younger, I managed to overcome my resistance to new things. After a short period of negativity, I flung myself at the Cuisinart food processor. I was curious about technology. I became a champion of e-mail and blogs—I found them romantic; I even made movies about them. But now I believe that almost anything new has been put on the earth in order to make me feel bad about my dwindling memory, and I've erected a wall to protect myself from most of it.

On the other side of that wall are many things, pinging. For the most part I pay no attention. For a long time, I didn't know the difference between the Sunnis and the Shias, but there were so many pings I was finally forced to learn. But I can't help wondering, Why did I bother? Wasn't it enough to know they didn't like each other? And in any case, I have now forgotten.

At this moment, some of the things I'm refusing to know anything about include:
The former Soviet republics
The Kardashians

Twitter
All Housewives, Survivors, American Idols,
    and Bachelors
Karzai's brother
Soccer
Monkfish
Jay-Z
Every drink invented since the Cosmopolitan
Especially the drink made with crushed mint
    leaves. You know the one.

I am going to Google the name of that drink. Be right back. . . .

The Mojito.

I am living in the Google years, no question of that. And there are advantages to it. When you forget something, you can whip out your iPhone and go to Google. The Senior Moment has become the Google moment, and it has a much nicer, hipper, younger, more contemporary sound, doesn't it? By handling the obligations of the search mechanism, you almost prove you can keep up. You can delude yourself that no one at the table thinks of you as a geezer. And finding the missing bit is so quick. There's none of the nightmare of the true Senior Moment—the long search for the answer, the guessing, the self-recrimination, the head-slapping mystification, the frustrated finger-snapping. You just go to Google and retrieve it.

You can't retrieve your life (unless you're on Wikipedia, in which case you can retrieve an inaccurate version of it).

But you can retrieve the name of that actor who was in that movie, the one about World War II. And the name of that writer who wrote that book, the one about her affair with that painter. Or the name of that song that was sung by that singer, the one about love.

You know the one.

Who Are You?

I Know You

I know you. I know you well. It's true I always have a little trouble with your name, but I do know your name. I just don't know it at this moment. We're at a big party. We've kissed hello. We've had a delightful conversation about how we are the last two people on the face of the earth who don't kiss on both cheeks. Now we're having a conversation about how phony all the people are who do kiss on both cheeks. Ha ha ha ha ha ha. You're so charming. If only I could remember your name. It's inexcusable that I can't. You've been to my house for dinner. I tried to read your last book. I know your girlfriend's name, or I almost know it. It's something like Chanelle. Only it's not. Chantelle? That's not it either. Fortunately, she isn't here, so I haven't forgotten both of your names. I'm becoming desperate. It's something like Larry. Is it Larry? No, it's not. Jerry? No, it's not. But it ends in a **Y.** Your last name: three syllables. Starts with a **C.** Starts with a **G?** I'm losing my mind. But a miracle occurs: the host is about to toast the guest of honor. Thank God. I can escape to the bar.

Have We Met?

Have we met? I think we've met. But I can't be sure. We were introduced, but I didn't catch your name because it's so noisy at this party. I'm going to assume we know each other, and I'm not going to say, "Nice to meet you." If I say, "Nice to meet you," I know what will happen. You'll say, "We've met." You'll say "We've met" in a sort of aggressive, irritable tone. And you won't even tell me your name so I can recover in some way. So I'm not going to say, "Nice to meet you." I'm going to say, "Nice to see you." I'll have a big smile on my face. I won't look desperate. But what I'll be thinking is, Please throw me your name. Please, please, please. Give me a hint. My husband is likely to walk up, and I'll have to introduce you, and I won't be able to, and you'll know that I have no idea who you are, even though we probably spent an entire weekend together on a boat in 1984. I have a secret signal with my husband that involves my pinching him very hard on the upper arm. The signal means, "Throw your name at this person because I have no idea whom I'm talking to." But my husband always forgets the secret signal and can't be counted on to respond to my pinching, even when it produces a bruise. I would like to chew my husband out about his forgetfulness on this point, but I'm not exactly in a position to do so since I myself have forgotten (if I ever knew it) the name of the person I'm talking to.

Old Friends

Old friends? We must be. You're delighted to see me. I'm delighted to see you. But who are you? Oh, my God, you're Ellen. I can't believe it. Ellen. "Ellen! How are you? It's been—how long has it been?" I'd like to suggest that the reason I didn't recognize you right off the bat is that you've done something to your hair, but you've done nothing to your hair, nothing that would excuse my not recognizing you. What you've actually done is gotten older. I don't believe it. You used to be my age, and now you're much, much, much older than I am. You could be my mother. Unless, of course, I look as old as you and I don't know it. Which is not possible. Or is it? I'm looking around the room and I notice that everyone in it looks like someone—and when I try to figure out exactly who that someone is, it turns out to be a former version of herself, a thinner version or a healthier version or a pre-plastic-surgery version or a taller version. If this is true of everyone, it must be true of me. Mustn't it? But never mind: you are speaking. "Maggie," you say, "it's been so long." "I'm not Maggie," I say. "Oh, my God," you say, "it's you. I didn't recognize you. You've done something to your hair."

Journalism: A Love Story

What I remember is that there was a vocational day during my freshman year in high school, and you had to choose which vocation you wanted to learn about. I chose journalism. I have no idea why. Part of the reason must have had to do with Lois Lane, and part with a wonderful book I'd been given one Christmas, called **A Treasury of Great Reporting.** The journalist who spoke at the vocational event was a woman sportswriter for the **Los Angeles Times.** She was very charming, and she mentioned in the course of her talk that there were very few women in the newspaper business. As I listened to her, I suddenly realized that I desperately wanted to be a journalist and that being a journalist was probably a good way to meet men.

So I can't remember which came first—wanting to be a journalist or wanting to date a journalist. The two thoughts were completely smashed up together.

I worked on the school newspaper in high school and college, and a week before graduating from Wellesley in 1962 I found a job in New York City. I'd gone to an employment agency on West Forty-second Street. I told the woman there that I wanted to be a journalist, and she said, "How would you like to work at **Newsweek** magazine?" and I said fine. She picked up the phone, made an appointment for me, and sent me right over to the Newsweek Building, at 444 Madison Avenue.

The man who interviewed me asked why I wanted to work at **Newsweek.** I think I was supposed to say something like, "Because it's such an important magazine," but I had no real feelings about the magazine one way or another. I had barely read **Newsweek**; in those days, it was a sorry second to **Time.** So I responded by saying that I wanted to work there because I hoped to become a writer. I was quickly assured that women didn't become writers at **Newsweek.** It would never have crossed my mind to object, or to say, "You're going to turn out to be wrong about me." It was a given in those days that if you were a woman and you wanted to do certain things, you were going to have to be the exception to the rule. I was hired as a mail girl, for $55 a week.

I'd found an apartment with a college friend at 110 Sullivan Street, a horrible brand-new white-brick building between Spring and Prince. The rent was $160 a month, with the first two months free. The real estate broker assured us that the South Village was a coming neighborhood, on the verge of being red-hot. This turned out not to be true for at least twenty years, by which time the area was called SoHo, and I was long gone. Anyway, I packed up a rental car on graduation day and set off to New York. I got lost only once—I had no idea you weren't supposed to take the George Washington Bridge to get to Manhattan. I remember being absolutely terrified when I realized that I was accidentally on the way to New Jersey and might never find a way to make a U-turn; I would drive south forever and never reach the city I'd dreamed of getting back to ever since I was five, when my parents had thoughtlessly forced me to move to California.

When I finally got to Sullivan Street, I discovered that the Festival of St. Anthony was taking place.

There was no parking on the block—they were frying zeppole in front of my apartment. I'd never heard of zeppole. I was thrilled. I thought the street fair would be there for months, and I could eat all the cotton candy I'd ever wanted. Of course it was gone the next week.

There were no mail boys at **Newsweek,** only mail girls. If you were a college graduate (like me) who had worked on your college newspaper (like me) and you were a girl (like me), they hired you as a mail girl. If you were a boy (unlike me) with exactly the same qualifications, they hired you as a reporter and sent you to a bureau somewhere in America. This was unjust but it was 1962, so it was the way things were.

My job couldn't have been more prosaic: mail girls delivered the mail. This was a long time ago, when there was a huge amount of mail, and it arrived in large sacks all day long. I was no mere mail girl, though; I was the Elliott girl. This meant that on Friday nights I worked late, delivering copy back and forth from the writers to the editors, one of whom was named Osborn Elliott, until it was very late. We often worked until three in the morning on Friday nights, and then we had to be back at work early Saturday, when the Nation and Foreign departments closed. It was exciting in its own self-absorbed way, which is very much the essence of journalism: you truly come to believe that you are living in the center of the universe and that the world out there is on tenterhooks waiting for the next copy of whatever publication you work at.

There were telex machines in a glass-enclosed area adjacent to the lobby, and one of my jobs was to rip off the telexes, which usually contained dispatches from the reporters in the bureaus, and deliver them to the writers and editors. One night a telex arrived concerning the owner of **Newsweek,** Philip Graham. I had seen Graham on several occasions. He was a tall, handsome guy's guy whose photographs never conveyed his physical attractiveness or masculinity; he would walk through the office, his voice booming, cracking jokes and smiling a great white toothy grin. He was in a manic phase of his manic depression, but no one knew this; no one even knew what manic depression was.

Graham had married Katharine Meyer, whose father owned **The Washington Post,** and he now ran **The Post** and the publishing empire that controlled **Newsweek.** But according to the telex, he was in the midst of a crack-up and was having a very public affair with a young woman who worked for **Newsweek.** He had misbehaved at some event or other and had used the word "fuck" in the course of it all. It was a big deal to say the word "fuck" in that era. This is one of the things that drives me absolutely crazy when I see movies that take place in the fifties and early sixties; people are always saying "fuck" in them. Trust me, no one threw that word around then the way they do now. I'll tell you something else: they didn't drink wine then. Nobody knew about wine. I mean, someone did, obviously, but most people drank hard liquor all the way through dinner. Recently I saw a movie in which people were eating take-out pizza in 1948 and it drove me nuts. There was no take-out pizza in 1948. There was barely any pizza, and barely any takeout. These are some of the things I know, and they're entirely useless, and take up way too much space in my brain.

Philip Graham's nervous breakdown—which ended finally in his suicide—was constantly under whispered discussion by the editors, and because I read all the telexes and was within earshot, even of whispers, I was riveted. There was a morgue—a library of clippings that was available for research— at **Newsweek**; morgues are one of the great joys of working in journalism. I went to it and pulled all the clips about Graham and read them between errands. I was fascinated by the story of this wildly attractive man and the rich girl he'd married. Years later, in Kay Graham's autobiography, I read their letters and realized that they'd once been in love, but as I went through the clips, I couldn't imagine it. It seemed clear he was an ambitious young man who'd made a calculated match with a millionaire's daughter. Now the marriage was falling apart, before my very eyes. It was wildly dramatic, and it almost made up for the fact that I was doing entirely menial work.

After a few months, I was promoted to the next stage of girldom at **Newsweek**: I became a clipper. Being a clipper entailed clipping newspapers from around the country. We all sat at something called the Clip Desk, armed with rip sticks and grease pencils, and we ripped up the country's newspapers and routed the clips to the relevant departments. For instance, if someone cured cancer in St. Louis, we sent the clipping to the Medicine section. Being a clipper was a horrible job, and to make matters worse, I was good at it. But I learned something: I became familiar with every major newspaper in America. I can't quite point out what good that did me, but I'm sure it did. Years later, when I got involved with a columnist from **The Philadelphia Inquirer,** I at least knew what his newspaper looked like.

Three months later, I was promoted again, this time to the highest rung: I became a researcher. "Researcher" was a fancy word—and not all that fancy at that—for "fact-checker," and that's pretty much what the job consisted of. I worked in the Nation Department. I was extremely happy to be there. This was not a bad job six months out of college; what's more, I'd been a political science major, so I was working in a field I knew something about. There were six writers and six researchers in the department, and we worked from Tuesday to Saturday night, when the magazine closed. For most of the week, none of us did anything. The writers waited for files from the reporters in the bureaus, which didn't turn up until Thursday or Friday. Then, on Friday afternoon, they all wrote their stories and gave them to us researchers to check. We checked a story by referring to whatever factual material existed; occasionally we made a phone call or did some minor reporting. Newsmagazine writers in those days were famous for using the expression "tk," which stood for "to come"; they were always writing sentences like, "There are tk lightbulbs in the chandelier in the chamber of the House of Representatives," and part of your job as a researcher was to find out just how many lightbulbs there were. These tidbits were not so much facts as factoids, but they were the way newsmagazines separated themselves from daily newspapers; the style reached an apotheosis in the work of Theodore H. White, a former **Time** writer, whose **Making of the President** books were filled with information about things like President Kennedy's favorite soup. (Tomato, with a glop of sour cream.) (I ate it for years, as a result.)

At **Newsweek,** when you had checked the facts and were convinced they were accurate, you underlined the sentence. You were done checking a piece when every word in it had been underlined. One Tuesday morning, we all arrived at work and discovered a gigantic crisis: one of the Nation stories in that week's **Newsweek** had been published with a spelling error—Konrad Adenauer's first name was spelled with a **C** instead of a **K.** The blame fell not to the writer (male) who had first misspelled the name, or to the many senior editors (male) and copy editors (male) who had edited the story, but to the two researchers (female) who'd checked it. They had been confronted, and were busy having an argument over which of them had underlined the word "Conrad." "That is not my underlining," one of them was saying.

With hindsight, of course, I can see how brilliantly institutionalized the sexism was at **Newsweek.** For every man, an inferior woman. For every male writer, a female drone. For every flamboyant inventor of a meaningless-but-unknown detail, a young drudge who could be counted on to fill it in. For every executive who erred, an underling to pin it on. But it was way too early in the decade for me to notice that, and besides, I was starting to realize that I was probably never going to be promoted to writer at **Newsweek.** And by the way, if I ever had been, I have no reason to think I would have been good at it.

The famous 114-day newspaper strike (which wasn't a strike but a lockout) began in December 1962, and one of its side effects was that several journalists who were locked out by their newspapers came to **Newsweek** to be writers, temporarily. One of them was Charles Portis, a reporter from the **New York Herald Tribune** whom I went out with for a while, but that's not the point (although it's not entirely beside the point); the point is that Charlie, who was a wonderful writer with a spectacular and entirely eccentric style (he later became a novelist and the author of **True Grit**), was no good at all at writing the formulaic, voiceless, unbylined stories with strict line counts that **Newsweek** printed.

By then I had become friends with Victor Navasky. He was the editor of a satirical magazine called **Monocle,** and it seemed that he knew everyone. He knew important people, and he knew people he made you think were important simply because he knew them. **Monocle** came out only sporadically, but it hosted a lot of parties, and I met people there who became friends for life, including Victor's wife, Annie, Calvin Trillin, and John Gregory Dunne. Victor also introduced me to Jane Green, who was an editor at Condé Nast. She was an older woman, about twenty-five, very stylish and sophisticated, and she knew everyone too. She introduced me to my first omelette, my first Brie, and my first vitello tonnato. She used the word "painterly" and tried to explain it to me. She asked me what kind of Jew I was. I had never heard of the concept of what kind of Jew you were. Jane was a German Jew, which was not to say she was from Germany but that her grandparents had been. She was extremely pleased about it. I had no idea it mattered. (And by the way, it didn't, really; those days were over.)

I could go on endlessly about the things I learned from Jane. She told me all about de Kooning and took me to the Museum of Modern Art to see pop art and op art. She taught me the difference between Le Corbusier and Mies van der Rohe. She'd gone out with a number of well-known journalists and writers, and long before I met them I knew, because of Jane, a number of intimate details about them. Eventually, I went to bed with one of them and that was the end of my friendship with her, but that's getting ahead of things.

One day after the newspaper strike was about a month old, Victor called to say he'd managed to raise $10,000 to put out parodies of the New York newspapers, and asked if I would write a parody of Leonard Lyons' gossip column in the **New York Post.** I said yes, although I had no idea what to do. I'd met Lyons—he appeared nightly at Sardi's, where my parents often had dinner when they were

27

in New York—but I'd never really focused on his column. I called my friend Marcia, who'd recently babysat Leonard Lyons' son's dogs, and asked her what the deal was with Lyons. She explained to me that the Lyons column was a series of short anecdotes with no point whatsoever. I went upstairs to the morgue at **Newsweek** and read a few weeks' worth of Lyons' columns and wrote the parody. Parodies are very odd things. I've written only about a half dozen of them in my life; they come on you like the wind, and you write them almost possessed. It's as close as a writer gets to acting—it's almost as if you're in character for a short time, and then it passes.

The papers Victor produced—the **New York Pest** and the **Dally News**—made their way to the newsstands, but they didn't sell. Newsstand dealers really didn't understand parodies in those days—this was long before **National Lampoon** and **The Onion**—and most of them sent them back to the distributor. But everyone in the business read them. They were funny. The editors of the **Post** wanted to sue, but the publisher, Dorothy Schiff, said, "Don't be ridiculous. If they can parody the **Post** they can write for it. Hire them." So the editors called Victor and Victor called me and asked if I'd be interested in trying out for a job at the **Post**. Of course I was.

I went down to the **Post** offices on West Street a

few days later. It was a freezing day in February and I got lost trying to find the entrance to the building, which was actually on Washington Street. I took the elevator to the second floor and walked down the long dingy hall and into the city room. I couldn't imagine I was in the right place. It was a large dusty room with dirty windows looking out at the Hudson, not that you could see anything through the windows. Sitting in a clump of desks in the winter dark was a group of three or four editors. They offered me a reporting tryout as soon as the lockout was over.

There were seven newspapers in New York at that time, and the **Post** was the least of them, circulation-wise. It had always been a liberal paper, and it had had glory days under an editor named James Wechsler, but those days were over. Still, the paper had a solid base of devoted readers. Seven weeks into the lockout, Dorothy Schiff bolted the Publishers Association and reopened the paper, and I took a two-week leave of absence from **Newsweek** and began my tryout. I'd prepared by studying the **Post**, but more important, by being coached by Jane, who'd worked there briefly. She explained everything I needed to know about the paper. She told me that the **Post** was an afternoon newspaper and the stories in it were known as "overnights"; they were not to be confused with the news stories in the morning papers. They were feature stories; they had a point of view; they were the reason people bought an afternoon paper in addition to a morning paper. You never used a simple "Who What Where Why When and How" lead in an afternoon paper. She also told me that when I got an assignment, never to say, "I don't understand" or "Where exactly is it?" or "How do I get in touch with them?" Go back to your desk, she said, and figure it out. Pull the clips from the morgue. Look in the telephone book. Look in the crisscross directory. Call your friends. Do anything but ask the editor what to do or how to get there.

I arrived for my tryout expecting the city room to look different from the way it had on that dark winter day I'd first come there, but except for brighter lighting, it didn't. It was a relic, really—a period set for a 1930s newsroom. The desks were old, the chairs were broken. Everyone smoked, but there were no ashtrays; the burning cigarettes rested on the edges of desks and left dark smudge marks. There were not enough desks to go around, so unless you'd been there for twenty years, you didn't have your own desk, or even a drawer; finding a place to sit was sort of like musical chairs. The windows were never cleaned. The doors leading into the city room had insets of frosted glass, and they were so dusty that someone had written the word "Philthy" on them with a finger. I couldn't have cared less. I had spent almost half my life wanting to be a newspaper reporter, and now I had a shot at it.

I had four bylines my first week. I interviewed the actress Tippi Hedren. I went to the Coney Island aquarium to write about two hooded seals that were refusing to mate. I interviewed an Italian film director named Nanni Loy. I covered a murder on West Eighty-second Street. On Friday afternoon, I was offered a permanent job at the paper. One of the reporters took me out for a drink that night, to a bar nearby called the Front Page. That's what it was called, the Front Page. Later that night, we took a taxi up Madison Avenue and we passed the Newsweek Building. I looked up at the eleventh floor, where the lights were ablaze, and I thought, Up there they are closing next week's edition of **Newsweek**, and nobody really gives a damn. It was a stunning revelation.

I loved the **Post**. Of course, it was a zoo. The editor was a sexual predator. The managing editor was a lunatic. Sometimes it seemed that half the staff was drunk. But I loved my job. In my first year there, I learned how to write, which I barely knew when I began. The editors and copy editors brought me along. They actually nurtured me. They assigned me short pieces at first, then longer pieces, then five-part series. I learned by doing, and after a while, I had an instinctive sense of structure. There was a brilliant copy editor, Fred McMorrow, who would walk my story back to me and explain why he was making the changes he was making. Never begin a story with a quote, he said. Never use anything but "said." Never put anything you really care about into the last paragraph because it will undoubtedly be cut for space. There was a great features editor, Joe Rabinovich, who kept my occasional stylistic excesses in line; he saved me from woeful idiocy when Tom Wolfe began writing for the **Herald Tribune** and I made a pathetic attempt to write exactly like him. The executive editor, Stan Opotowsky, came up with a series of offbeat feature assignments for me. I wrote about heat waves and cold snaps; I covered the Beatles and Bobby Kennedy and the Star of India robbery.

The **Post** had a bare-bones staff, but more women worked there than worked at all the other New York papers combined. The greatest of the rewrite men at the **Post** was a woman named Helen Dudar. **Hello, sweetheart, get me rewrite.** In those days, the **Post** published six editions a day, starting at eleven in the morning and ending with the four-thirty stock market final. When news broke, reporters in the street would phone in the details from pay phones and rewrite men would write the stories. The city room was right next to the press room, and the noise—of reporters typing, pressmen linotyping, wire machines clacking, and presses rolling—was a journalistic fantasy.

I worked at the **Post** for five years. Then I became a magazine writer. I believed in journalism. I believed in truth. I believed that when people claimed they'd been misquoted, they were just having trouble dealing with the sight of their words in cold, hard print. I believed that when political activists claimed that news organizations conspired against them, they had no idea that most journalistic enterprises were far too inept to harbor conspiracy. I believed that I was temperamentally suited to journalism because of my cynicism and emotional detachment; I sometimes allowed that these were character flaws, but I didn't really believe it.

I married a journalist, and that didn't work. But then I married another, and it did.

Now I know that there's no such thing as the truth. That people are constantly misquoted. That news organizations are full of conspiracy (and that, in any case, ineptness is a kind of conspiracy). That emotional detachment and cynicism get you only so far.

But for many years I was in love with journalism. I loved the city room. I loved the pack. I loved smoking and drinking scotch and playing dollar poker. I didn't know much about anything, and I was in a profession where you didn't have to. I loved the speed. I loved the deadlines. I loved that you wrapped the fish.

You can't make this stuff up, I used to say.

I'd known since I was a child that I was going to live in New York eventually, and that everything in between would be just an intermission. I'd spent all those years imagining what New York was going to be like. I thought it was going to be the most exciting, magical, fraught-with-possibility place that you could ever live; a place where if you really wanted something you might be able to get it; a place where I'd be surrounded by people I was dying to know; a place where I might be able to become the only thing worth being, a journalist.

And I'd turned out to be right.

The Legend

I grew up in Beverly Hills, in a Spanish house in the flats. My parents had a large group of friends, almost all of them transplanted New Yorkers who were in the business. That's what it was known as—the business. (People who were not in the business were known as civilians.) The men were screenwriters or television writers. Their wives did nothing. They were known at the time as housewives, but none of them did housework—they all had cooks and maids and laundresses. Our mother had household help too, but she was different: she worked. "You'll just have to tell them your mother can't be there because she has to work." My mother uttered that sentence several times a year; it was meant to get her off the hook for PTA meetings and such, but it was also meant to make us understand that she was a cut above the other mothers. She was even a cut above the other career women—there were a few in the business, including the costume designer Edith Head, whom my mother once took me to lunch with, but none of them had careers **and** children. My mother did. Also, she served delicious food, which was another way she liked to rub it in. And she could keep help. What's more, she dressed beautifully.

This was long before the concept of having it all, but my mother had it all. And then she ruined the narrative by becoming a crazy drunk. But that came later.

Every day my parents came home from work, and we all gathered in the den. My parents had drinks and there were crudités for us—although they were not called crudités at the time, they were called carrots and celery. Then we had dinner in the dining room. The plates were heated, and there were butter balls made with wooden paddles. There was an appetizer, a main course, and dessert. We thought everyone lived like this.

The Legend

At our dinner table, we discussed politics and what we were reading. We told cheerful stories of what had happened in school that day. We played charades. My mother, once a camp counselor, would lead us in song. "Under the spreading chestnut tree," we would sing, and we would spread our arms and bang our chests. Or we would sing, "The bells they all go tingalingaling," and we'd clink our spoons against our glasses. We learned to believe in Lucy Stone, the New Deal, Norman Thomas, and Edward R. Murrow. We were taught that organized religion was the root of all evil and that Adlai Stevenson was God. We were indoctrinated in my mother's rules: Never buy a red coat. Red meat keeps your hair from turning gray. You **can** leave the table but you **may not** leave the table. Girdles ruin your stomach muscles. The means and the end are the same.

And there were stories, the stories we grew up on. How my parents met and fell in love. How they ran away from the camp where they were counselors and got married so they could sleep in the same tent. How my mother's aunt Minnie became the first woman dentist in the history of the world. And finally—and this is where this is all leading—how my mother threw Lillian Ross out of our house.

This was not just a story, it was a legend.

It seemed that Lillian Ross had come to one of my

37

parents' parties. About once a year they had a big sit-down dinner for about forty people, with tables and chairs from Abbey Rents. They served their delicious food cooked by their longtime housekeeper, and my mother wore a Galanos dress bought for the occasion. All their friends were invited—Julius J. Epstein (**Casablanca**), Richard Maibaum (**The Big Clock** and, eventually, the Bond movies), Richard Breen (**Dragnet**), Charles Brackett (**Ninotchka, Sunset Boulevard**), and Albert Hackett and his wife, Frances Goodrich, who had the greatest credits of all (**The Thin Man, Seven Brides for Seven Brothers, It's a Wonderful Life, The Diary of Anne Frank**). I would stand on the second floor and look over the banister down at the parties, and listen to Herbie Baker (**The Girl Can't Help It**) play the piano after dinner. Once I caught a glimpse of Shelley Winters, who was dating Liam O'Brien (**Young at Heart**), and once Marge and Gower Champion turned up. That was as starry as it ever got.

One night, St. Clair McKelway was invited to one of my parents' parties. McKelway was a well-known **New Yorker** magazine writer who'd written a couple of movies. He called beforehand to ask if he could bring a friend, Lillian Ross. Did my mother know who she was? he asked. My mother certainly knew who she was. **The New Yorker** arrived by mail every week. Along with the Sunday **New York**

Times and **The Saturday Review of Literature,** it was required reading for the diaspora of smart people living in Hollywood; reading it made them feel they hadn't lost a step, that they could move back east at a moment's notice.

Lillian Ross was young at the time, but she was already famous for her reporting in **The New Yorker,** and for her ability to make her subjects sound like fools. She had just published her devastating profile of Ernest Hemingway and was in Los Angeles reporting her piece on John Huston and the making of **The Red Badge of Courage.** My mother told St. Clair McKelway that he was welcome to bring Lillian Ross to dinner but that Ross had to agree that the party would be off the record.

So Lillian Ross came to the party. Before dinner, she asked my mother for a tour of the house. My mother showed her around, and at a certain point, Ross came upon a picture of my three sisters and me.

"Are these your children?" she asked my mother.

"Yes," my mother said.

"Do you ever see them?" Lillian Ross asked.

That did it.

My mother walked Lillian Ross downstairs and back to McKelway.

"Out," she said.

And Lillian Ross and St. Clair McKelway left.

That was the legend of my mother and Lillian Ross. My mother loved to tell it. It was practically a cowboy movie. We'd been raised to believe that a woman could do everything and Lillian Ross had dared to question it. In our house. So my mother threw her out.

I loved this story. I loved all stories that proved that my mother was right and everyone else was wrong, especially since there was a piece of me that couldn't help wishing she was exactly like everyone else's mother.

It was at least ten years before I began to wonder about it. Had it ever actually happened? There are all sorts of stories you grow up with, and then you get older, and there's just something about them that doesn't pass the nose test. They're somehow too perfect. And the most nagging part is the coup de grâce, the perfectly chosen last line. My father wrote a memoir once, and in it are several completely unbelievable episodes in which he tells people like Darryl Zanuck to go fuck themselves. This legend of my mother and Lillian Ross was in some way a version of those stories. It was too good to be true.

My mother became an alcoholic when I was fifteen. It was odd. One day she wasn't an alcoholic, and the next day she was a complete lush. She drank a bottle of scotch every night. Around midnight she would come flying out of her bedroom, banging and screaming and terrorizing us all. My father drank too, but he was a sloppy, sentimental drunk, and somehow his alcoholism was more benign.

By the time I went off to Wellesley, their movie work had dried up, but somehow they were sober enough in the daytime to collaborate; they wrote a successful play called **Take Her, She's Mine,** about a Southern California family whose daughter goes off to an eastern women's college. It quoted the letters I'd written from college, and it opened on Broadway during my senior year, starring Art Carney as the father and Elizabeth Ashley as the daughter. Everyone at Wellesley knew about it and about my remarkable mother, the writer who could do everything.

I didn't expect either of my parents to turn up at my graduation, but a few days before it, my mother called to say she'd decided to come. She arrived in all her stylish glory. She wore her suit, and her three-inch heels, and her clip-on earrings that matched her brooch. She slept in the dormitory, in the room next to mine, for two nights. I lay in my bed and listened through the paper-thin wall to her drunken mutterings. I was terrified that she'd burst from her room into the halls of Tower Court and mortify me in front of my classmates, that she'd stagger down the hall banging and screaming, and my friends would learn the truth.

But what was the truth?

I was invested in the original narrative; I was a true believer. My mother was a goddess.

But my mother was an alcoholic.

Alcoholic parents are so confusing. They're your parents, so you love them; but they're drunks, so you hate them. But you love them. But you hate them. They have moments when they're still the people you grew up idolizing; they have moments when you can't imagine they were ever anything but monsters. And then, after a while, they're monsters full-time. The people they used to be have enormous power over you—it will be forty years before you buy a red coat (and even then, you will wear it only once)—but the people they've turned into have no power over you at all.

For a long time before she died, I wished my mother were dead. And then she died, and it wasn't one of those things where I thought, Why did I think that? What was wrong with me? What kind of person would wish her mother dead? No, it wasn't one of those things at all. My mother had become a complete nightmare. She drank herself to death at the age of fifty-seven.

I was thirty when she died. After five years as a newspaper reporter, I'd become a freelance magazine writer. I wrote for **Esquire** in the last days of editor Harold Hayes and for **New York** magazine in the first days of Clay Felker. It was a heady time. Magazines like **Esquire** and **New York** were the zeitgeist, and the (mostly) men who wrote for them were cocky and full of beans. They thought they had invented nonfiction, which they hadn't, and they even thought they had invented hanging out together in restaurants and staying up late. It was an era when people really cared about magazines, when the arrival of a new **Esquire** on the newsstands was a bombshell, and it was seriously fun to be part of it. I became an **Esquire** writer. I wrote a column there, about women. In the world of print, the small world where I lived, I became a little bit famous.

I had never met Lillian Ross, but I wondered about her from time to time. I'd read all her early work and admired it greatly, but she'd stopped doing bylined profiles and wrote mostly unsigned "Talk of the Town" pieces in **The New Yorker.** She was rumored to be having an affair with the editor of the magazine, William Shawn, and she seemed (from a distance) to have fallen under the evil spell of blandness that he'd cast over the magazine.

At the time, there was a cold war in the magazine world, between those of us at **Esquire** and **New York,** and those of them at **The New Yorker.** They lived enviable lives—they had contracts and health insurance, and they could take months writing pieces; we, on the other hand, were always overextended and scrambling for dough. They were feigning modesty and disdaining success; we were self-aggrandizing and climbing the greasy pole. They were the anointed; we were pagans. They worshipped the famously reclusive "Mr. Shawn," and they dropped his name in hushed tones as if he were the Ba'al Shem Tov; we, on the other hand, jumped from Harold to Clay and back again. They thought we were egomaniacs; we thought they were weird.

I was the sort of person Lillian Ross would hate, if she even knew who I was, or so it seemed to me one night in 1978 when I was pulled across a room to meet her. I was at a party at the home of Lorne Michaels, the producer of **Saturday Night Live.** Lillian Ross had been reporting a profile of Lorne for eight years. "You two must meet," Lorne was saying, as he brought us together. I could see in an instant that Lillian Ross did not share this imperative. "You have so much in common," he said, as he sat us down on the sofa.

"It's so nice to meet you," I said.

"And you," she said.

She was a tiny woman with short curly hair and bright blue eyes, and she smiled and waited for me to begin.

I had one goal: to find out if my mother's story was true and to find it out without giving anything away. I didn't want Lillian Ross to know that she was a character in our family saga, and I didn't want to betray my mother by giving away the fact that Ross had lingered on, in our home, for so many years after her cameo appearance there. I wanted my mother to win the duel, whether or not it had actually happened.

But how to ask the question? "Is it true my mother threw you out of the house?" seemed a little bold. "I think you once met my mother" seemed coy, especially if Ross remembered the incident.

I couldn't figure out what to do.

So I began by saying that I was a huge fan. She said thank you and waited for me to say something else. I took this to mean she'd never read anything I'd written, or that she hated my work, or perhaps— I was reaching for straws here—she had no idea that I was a writer.

I asked her about her son and I told her about mine. It's my experience that no one but your very close friends is truly interested in your children, but we went on pretending for a while.

Then I asked her if she was still writing the profile of Lorne, as I'd heard. Yes, she said, she was. Another pause. It was clear that Lillian Ross was not even going to meet me halfway. I was starting to become irritated. Was it true that she was now in her eighth year of writing about Lorne, I asked. Yes, she was, she said. When do you think you'll be done with it, I asked. I asked this in what I hoped was an innocent manner, but I didn't fool her. She had no idea, she replied. We don't have to rush things at **The New Yorker.**

That cleared up one thing: she knew who I was.

I plowed on: I asked her why she'd stopped writing signed profiles. I asked the question cleverly, I thought. Honey dripped from my lips. I said I had loved her long pieces so much and missed reading them and wondered why she had stopped writing them. She replied that she'd stopped writing bylined articles because she believed that too much magazine journalism these days was egotistical and self-promoting.

I had to hand it to her: that was good.

And then Lillian Ross answered the question I hadn't asked.

"I went to your house once," she said. "I met your mother."

"Really?" I said, feigning absolute ignorance.

"Didn't see much of you though," she said.

So there it was.

No question.

It had happened.

I have met Lillian Ross many times since that night. She still writes for **The New Yorker,** although **The New Yorker** no longer publishes unsigned pieces. She eventually wrote a first-person confessional about her relationship with Mr. Shawn, so on some level she threw off the veil. I consider her to be as egotistical and self-promoting as the rest of us, and that's a compliment.

But this is not about Lillian Ross, really. It's about my mother. Long before she died, I'd given up on her. But that night with Lillian Ross, I got her back; I got back the mother I'd idolized before it had all gone to hell. I got back the simple version. She'd thrown Lillian Ross out of our house for all the right reasons. The legend was true.

My Aruba

I am sorry to report that I have an Aruba.

You don't know what an Aruba is, but you're about to find out.

My Aruba is named after the Caribbean island of Aruba, where the winds are so strong that all the little trees on it are blown sideways in one direction. But my Aruba is not an island. It's the thing that's happening with my hair, on the crown of my head, in the back. My cowlicks have won, and they are all blown sideways, leaving a little bare space. It's not a bald spot exactly. It's there when I wake up; then I fix my hair and make it go away; and then, a couple of hours later, it's back again. A gust of wind, a short walk, a ride on the subway, or life itself—anything at all can make my hair blow sideways, leaving a spot on the back of my head where my scalp is showing through.

And the thing is, I can't see it.

Even if I catch a glimpse of myself in a window, it's not visible because it's in the back.

I look fine from the front.

I look as young as a person can look given how old I am.

But from the back, it looks as if I have either forgotten to comb my hair or as if I am just a little bit bald.

Neither of these things is true, I swear.

But what is true is that I am older than I look, and my Aruba is a sign. I did not have one when I was younger, but now I do.

This is not the worst thing about getting older, but it's very disheartening. And almost no one tells you you've got one at the time.

There are a whole bunch of things no one tells you about and then you come home and discover you've been walking around all day with them. I am of course referring to spinach in your teeth, or a tag that's sticking up the back of your collar, or a fluffy piece of toilet paper on your shoe. I am talking about those little dark flecks that sometimes end up in the corners of your eyes, and mascara that has run. I'm talking about lint.

It's very sad to look in the bathroom mirror at the end of an evening and realize you've spent the last ninety minutes with spinach on your tooth. Or parsley, which is an even more dangerous thing to eat. And that none of your friends loved you enough to tell you.

This is especially painful because it's so easy to tell people they have spinach in their teeth. All you have to do is say, "You have spinach in your teeth."

But what can you say to a person who has an Aruba, especially since, until I wrote this piece, there was no word to describe it?

But now that I have come up with the term, I would appreciate your telling me whenever I have an Aruba. Because then I can fix it. Temporarily, anyway.

My Life as an Heiress

I never knew why my mother wasn't close to her brother Hal. I can guess. It's possible that he didn't help out financially with their parents. It's possible that she didn't like his wife, Eleanor. It's possible that she resented forever the fact that her parents found the money to send him to Columbia but made her go to a public college. Who knows? The secret is dead and buried.

In any case, I grew up without meeting my uncle Hal. We lived in Los Angeles, and Hal lived in Washington, D.C., with the aforementioned Eleanor. They were both government economists, and then, in the fifties, they quit. There were rumors of left-wing affiliations. My parents had never been further to the left than socialism, but these were the blacklist years. They knew a dozen people who had named names, and they also knew at least two of the Hollywood Ten, plus several they claimed would have gone to jail, along with the Ten, had there been Eleven, or Twelve. My parents were worried that rumors of Hal and Eleanor's left-wing affiliations would reach all the way to California and bite them, and apparently that was exactly what happened, although without any real damage. One day in the early fifties they were called into the office of Spyros Skouras, an old Greek who was then running Twentieth Century Fox. Skouras waved a piece of paper about Hal at my mother and said, "Phoebe, vy you a Communist?" My mother explained to Skouras she was not her brother Hal, and not a Communist, and that was pretty much the end of it, except as an anecdote.

By the time I was in college, Uncle Hal and Aunt Eleanor were no longer anywhere near communism, if they'd ever been: they were in real estate, and they were very, very rich. In 1961, when I was working in Washington on a college political internship, they took me to Duke Zeibert's for dinner. Hal was a sweet, lovely man, and Eleanor was a pistol. She had a longish, horsy face and blondish hair and she loved a laugh. On weekends I would go stay at their house in Falls Church, a splendid new place they'd just built as part of a large development. Eleanor and Hal had no children, but they had lots of houses—they bought them and sold them, without looking back. They owned art, and Chinese antiquities, and Persian rugs, and their house was run, nicely, by a housekeeper named Louise. I mention Louise for a reason, as you will see.

My parents were really not into family—I'd never met my father's brothers or my first cousins—but Hal and Eleanor were in touch with all sorts of people on my mother's side of things, and that summer in Washington they introduced me to some of my mother's relatives who were my second or third cousins, depending on how you count. One was Joe Borkin, a well-known Washington lawyer who was an expert in the family antecedents and couldn't believe I'd grown up with no idea where my maternal grandparents were born; he told me, and, out of loyalty to my mother, who had no interest in such things, I promptly forgot. Another was Morty Plotkin, a doctor with no bedside manner whatsoever who had wisely gone into radiology. He was married to Tedda, whose name I was deeply fond of. Tedda Plotkin. You've got to love that name. Years later, when my mother was dying of cirrhosis, Tedda called me out of the blue and yelled at me, as if it were all my fault. Hal and Eleanor also introduced me to Eleanor's nephew Irwin the dentist, who eventually went into business with Eleanor and Hal. I mention him for a reason too.

After college, I moved to New York, and every so often Hal and Eleanor would come to town and take me to lunch or dinner. When I married my first husband, they gave us a large antique gilt candelabrum that I vaguely recall they claimed was Louis Quatorze. This cannot be true. After my divorce, Hal called to make sure my husband hadn't walked off with it.

That candelabrum came with me to my apartment in the East Fifties, and then to my second marriage, where I distinctly remember it sitting, looking idiotic, in the garage in Bridgehampton. Where is it today, I wonder. I would really like to know, because it was fabulous and I'm finally old enough to appreciate it. No doubt it was a casualty of divorce. When you get divorced and you don't get the house (which I never did), you leave behind all sorts of things you don't have the sense to know you'll someday wonder about, or wish you still had, or, worst of all, feel genuinely nostalgic for.

In 1974, Eleanor died. Years passed. I saw Uncle Hal in Washington and New York. My father and he were both widowers, they spoke on the phone from time to time, and afterward my father would call to bring me up to date. My father by then was in the early stages of forgetting things, but one thing he never forgot was a phone number, and in his later years he made at least a hundred phone calls a day, all of them brief. He never said hello and he never said good-bye. He didn't give anyone a chance to say, "I'm busy" or "Lose my number" or "I don't have time to talk." He came right to the point and then, as my sister Delia wrote in her book **Hanging Up,** he hung up.

"I've just written my memoirs," he would say, "and I'm calling them **Me.**"

"Great," I would say.

He would hang up.

"I just called Kate Hepburn and I told her the name of my memoirs," he would say. "She loved it."

"That's great, Dad."

He would hang up.

I always hoped that he would show some interest in my kids, Max and Jacob, but he didn't even remember their names. One day Jacob answered the phone and my father said: "Is this Abraham or the other one?" I consider it a testament to Jacob that at the age of seven, he knew it was funny. Still, it made me sad. You always think that a bolt of lightning is going to strike and your parents will magically change into the people you wish they were, or back into the people they used to be. But they're never going to. And even though you know they're never going to, you still hope they will.

My father's bulletins about my uncle Hal were never about Hal himself but about Hal's vast estate, which, according to my father, was being left entirely to my three sisters and me.

"I talked to Hal and you're in the will," he would say.

"You're still in the will," he would say.

"Four-way split among you four girls," he would say.

"Big bucks," he would say.

My father had minimal credibility at that point in my life, so it never crossed my mind to think that he was telling the truth, that I was going to be the recipient of inherited wealth. And Uncle Hal was in fine health. But then, one summer day in 1987, as I sat at my desk struggling with a screenplay I was writing in order to pay the bills, the phone rang; it was an administrator at a Washington, D.C., hospital, calling to say that Hal was dying of pneumonia and I should, as his next of kin, be prepared to make an end-of-life decision. I hung up, stunned. The phone rang again. It was Tedda Plotkin, wife of the radiologist, calling me, for the second time in my life, to say that Hal's apartment in Washington was full of extremely valuable rugs and art and I should have it padlocked immediately or else Louise the housekeeper might run off with everything in it. I told Tedda that I seriously doubted Louise would do anything of the kind, but that she'd worked for Hal and Eleanor for most of her adult life and she was welcome to run off with anything she wanted. The phone rang again. It was the hospital. Hal had died.

I called my sister Delia. "Prepare to be an heiress," I said.

Neither Delia nor I had the slightest idea of what Hal's estate was worth. There were profits from the houses he and Eleanor had flipped, and from large developments they had built in McLean and Falls Church, block after block of upscale suburban dream homes with indoor pools and rec rooms and breakfast nooks and the like. And there was also the Famous Puerto Rican Thing. Hal and Eleanor had bought a huge parcel of land somewhere in Puerto Rico and had begun a development there, in part-nership with Irwin the dentist. Every so often I would ask Hal about it, and Hal would reply that it was coming along great, that he'd just been to Puerto Rico, that they were meeting with the archi-tect, that the plans were terrific, that they'd seen the models, that they were looking for more investors.

It seemed to me he had to have been worth at least $3 million. Which was a lot of money at the time. Divided by four it came out to $750,000 for each of us. I couldn't believe it. It was a fortune. It would change everything. Okay, maybe it was only $2 million. That would still be a half million each. On the other hand, perhaps it was four. A million dollars each. A million dollars each! I kept estimating, and dividing by four, and mentally spending the money. My husband and I had recently bought a house on Long Island, and the renovation had cost much more than we'd ever dreamed. There was nothing left for landscaping. I went outside and walked around the house. I mentally planted several trees. I ripped out the scraggly lawn and imagined the huge trucks of sod I would now be able to pay for. I considered a trip to the nursery to look at hydrangeas. My heart was racing. I pulled my husband away from his work and we had a conversation about what kind of trees we wanted. A dogwood, definitely. A great big dogwood. It would cost a small fortune, and now we were about to have one.

I went upstairs and looked at the script I'd been writing. I would never have to work on it again. I was just doing it for the money and, let's face it, it was never going to get made, and besides, it was really hard. I shut down the computer. I lay down on the bed to think about other ways to spend Uncle Hal's money. It crossed my mind that we needed a new headboard.

Thus, in fifteen minutes, did I pass through the first two stages of inherited wealth: Glee and Sloth.

The phone rang.

It was my father. "Hal died," he said.

"I know," I said.

"He was leaving his money to the four of you," my father went on, "but I told him to cut you out of the will because you already have enough money."

"What?" I said.

He hung up.

I couldn't believe it.

I looked outside at the lawn. So much for the sod.

I called Delia. "Wait till you hear this development," I said, and told her what had happened.

"Well, we'll just even it out," Delia said. "We'll each give you whatever percentage of what we inherit and that will make it fair."

"One-fourth," I said.

"You were always better at math," she said. "I will call the others."

She called the others and called me back.

"Amy is willing," she said. "Hallie is not."

I couldn't believe it. The four of us had always had an agreement that if any one of us was cut out of my father's will, the others would cut her back in. Surely that applied to Uncle Hal too.

The day was not even over, and we had entered the third stage of inherited wealth: Dissension.

The next day I got a phone call from Hal's lawyer. My father had turned out to be wrong: Hal had not cut me out of his will after all. He had left half his estate to the four of us, and the other half to Louise the housekeeper.

I was happy for Louise. She deserved the money.

As for me, I was down to one-eighth. Not as good as one-fourth, but if the estate turned out to be four million dollars, it was still a bundle of money.

"How much money is there?" I asked the lawyer.

"Not much," he said.

"Not much meaning what?" I said.

"Less than half a million," he said.

Way less than a half million, it turned out. Thanks to Irwin the dentist, Hal had lost almost all his money in the Puerto Rican adventure. What was left, divided by eight, would buy sod, but it was not going to rescue me from the screenplay I was writing.

"The good news," the lawyer said, "is that if you inherit less than sixty-eight thousand dollars, there's no inheritance tax."

I called Delia and Amy and told them. I didn't call Hallie. I was never speaking to my sister Hallie again.

I went upstairs and turned on my computer and went back to work.

The next week my sister Amy called to say that

she had heard from Hal's lawyer that there might be a Monet. There was a painting in the closet, and they were sending it to the appraiser. By then, I had ceased hoping, but it didn't stop Amy from entering the fourth stage of inherited wealth: The Possible Masterpiece in the Closet.

I probably don't need to tell you that it was not a Monet.

In the end, the four of us inherited about $40,000 each from Uncle Hal.

So I never did enter the fifth stage of inherited wealth: Wealth.

I finished the screenplay and it got made. I am quick to draw lessons from my own experience, and the lesson I drew from this one was that I was extremely lucky not to have ever inherited real money, because I might not have finished writing **When Harry Met Sally,** which changed my life.

When Harry Met Sally was a huge hit and it even went into profit. We bought a dogwood. It's really beautiful. It blooms in late June, and it reminds me of my sweet Uncle Hal.

Going to the Movies

We went to the movies the other night. We live in New York City, where it costs $13.00 to see a movie, which doesn't include the $1.50 surcharge for buying the tickets ahead of time online. I love buying tickets ahead of time online. One of the genuine miracles of modern life, as far as I'm concerned, is that moment when you enter a movie theater and stick your credit card into a machine, and it spits the exact tickets you ordered straight out at you. Every single time it happens, I just want to say, "I don't believe it! This is great!! Wow!!!"

On the other hand, it turns out that there's a new technological advance in the buying-tickets-ahead-of-time department that takes all the fun out of it: you can now print out your confirmation at home, skip the machine, and go straight to the ticket taker. The ticket taker then scans your printout and prints the tickets right at the entrance to the theater, thus holding up all the people behind you on the ticket line and entirely eliminating the one miraculous moment you used to be able to count on when going to see a movie.

But the other night, as it turned out, we didn't have to give our printout to the ticket taker, because when we walked into the theater, there was no ticket taker. The entrance to the theater was completely empty of personnel. The other customers just walked right in without giving their tickets to any-one, and we did too. We trooped two flights down-stairs to Theater 7, expecting to bump into a ticket taker on our way to the theater, but we never did. We had also hoped to buy something at the refreshment counter, but the lower-level refreshment counter was closed and the popcorn was just sitting there, getting stale, in a big cold pile.

I should probably say at this point that the theater we went to was the Loews Orpheum 7, which is located at Eighty-sixth Street and Third Avenue in Manhattan. I should probably also say that the Loews Orpheum 7 is owned by AMC, but it used to be owned by Loews Cineplex Entertainment Corporation, and when it was, I was on the board of directors of Loews. This was a sad experience in my life, because I had modestly hoped, in my role as a board member, to do something about the unbelievably low quality of the food sold in movie theaters. As it turned out, no one at Loews cared about what I thought about the food sold in movie theaters. So I dutifully attended the board meetings and was subjected to a series of PowerPoint presentations that were meant to validate the company's then-policy of building costly, large cineplexes, most of them conveniently located right across the street from other costly, large cineplexes being built by rival theater companies.

One day, about two years into my tenure, I was staying in Los Angeles, in a hotel, and I attended a Loews board meeting by telephone; it was so boring that I decided to put the call on hold and go get a manicure downstairs. When I got back to my room, only twenty minutes later, and picked up the receiver, everyone was screaming at one another. I didn't want to admit that I had left the room—and by the way, no one had even noticed—so I listened for a while and realized that while I'd been out having my nails done, the company had gone bankrupt.

This was a shock to me and to everyone else on the board. I never did find out why the news hadn't been mentioned earlier in the board meeting, but that, of course, was one of the reasons everyone was screaming at one another: there were people on the board whose companies owned shares in Loews Corporation who had just found out that they'd lost hundreds of millions of dollars as a result of a bankruptcy no one had even had the courtesy to warn them about. It wasn't even on the agenda!

A few months later, a Canadian businessman bought Loews Theatres at a bargain-basement price and then sold it to AMC, which as far as I can tell has done nothing whatsoever to improve the food sold at the refreshment counter or anything else. I mean, it used to be so romantic to go to a movie—to sit in a great big theater that had a balcony, and boxes, and fabulous gilt trim on the walls, and a big red velvet curtain. Now we go to horrible unadorned gray rectangles where the sound bleeds in from the gray rectangle right next door. It's sad.

Anyway, the other night. We passed the shuttered refreshment counter, went into the theater, and sat down. The ads were already playing. There was a diet cola ad that was so in love with itself that it actually recommended going to a special Web site that explained how the ad had been made. There was an ad for buying tickets ahead of time online. Then, suddenly, the sound turned off and the screen went completely dark. Several minutes passed. The theater was three-quarters full, but no one moved. In some strange and inexplicable way, I felt responsible. I stood up and went two flights upstairs. A ticket taker had materialized and was now taking tickets. I told her that the system in Theater 7 had shut down. She looked at me blankly. I asked her if she would tell someone that the system had shut down. She said she would and went on taking tickets. After a couple of minutes, when the customers had all passed through, she yelled out, "Projection, is there something wrong in Theater Seven?" I went back downstairs.

The system started up again. A trailer began to play. I noticed that there was a large band of white light across the bottom of the screen, and that the images of the actors that were being projected were all cut off in the middle of their eyeballs.

I left the theater and walked upstairs again. The ticket taker was still there, taking tickets. I asked her if she would ask the projectionist to reframe the movie. Once again she looked at me blankly, so I asked again. She promised she would. I waited until she walked off in the direction of the unseen projectionist. By the time I got back to my seat, the image on-screen had been reframed, although not perfectly, but by then I was too exhausted by my heroism to complain further.

Going to the Movies

The movie began. It was out of sync, but hey, it was a good movie. And it was only **slightly** out of sync. Besides, there was a huge amount of cutting and action, so you could sort of live with its being out of sync. Then, in the last twenty minutes, the movie became unbelievably, noticeably, extraordinarily out of sync. But it was almost over. And I didn't want to leave my seat for fear I might miss something.

Afterward, on my way out of the theater, I asked if I could speak to the theater manager. She turned out to be on maternity leave. I asked if I could speak to the assistant manager. There was no assistant manager on duty. So I ended up with my old friend, the ticket taker, who was, as you can imagine, thrilled to see me again. I told her that the last reel of the movie we had just seen was out of sync and that they might want to fix it before the next show began. She promised me they would.

Twenty-five Things
People Have a Shocking
Capacity to Be Surprised by
Over and Over Again

1. Journalists sometimes make things up.
2. Journalists sometimes get things wrong.
3. Almost all books that are published as memoirs were initially written as novels, and then the agent/editor said, This might work better as a memoir.
4. Beautiful young women sometimes marry ugly, old rich men.
5. In business, there is no such thing as synergy in the good sense of the term.

6. Freedom of the press belongs to the man who owns one.
7. Nothing written in today's sports pages makes sense to anyone who didn't read yesterday's sports pages.
8. There is no explaining the stock market but people try.
9. The Democrats are deeply disappointing.
10. Movies have no political effect whatsoever.
11. Men cheat.
12. A lot of people take the Bible literally.
13. Pornography is the opiate of the masses.
14. You can never know the truth of anyone's marriage, including your own.
15. People actually sign prenuptial agreements.
16. Mary Matalin and James Carville are married.
17. Bagels don't taste as good as they used to.
18. Everybody lies.
19. The reason it's important for a Democrat to be president is the Supreme Court.
20. Howard Stern is apparently very nice in person.
21. In Manhattan a small one-bedroom apartment that needs work costs $1 million.
22. People look like their dogs.
23. Cary Grant was Jewish.
24. Cary Grant wasn't Jewish.
25. Larry King has never read a book.

I Just Want to Say:
The Egg-White Omelette

There's a new book out about diet, and it apparently says what I've known all my life—protein is good for you, carbohydrates are bad, and fat is highly overrated as a dangerous substance. Well, it's about time. As my mother used to say, you can never have too much butter.

For example, here's how we cook steak in our house: First you coat the steak in kosher salt. Then you cook the steak in a very hot frying pan. When it's done, you throw a huge pat of butter on top of it.

I Just Want to Say: The Egg-White Omelette

That's it. And by the way, I'm not talking about sweet butter, I'm talking about salted butter.

Here's another thing it says in this book: dietary cholesterol has nothing whatsoever to do with your cholesterol count. This is another thing I've known all my life, which is why you will not find me lying on my deathbed regretting not having eaten enough chopped liver. Let me explain this: You can eat all sorts of things that are high in dietary cholesterol (like lobster and avocado and eggs) and they have NO EFFECT WHATSOEVER on your cholesterol count. NONE. WHATSOEVER. DID YOU HEAR ME? I'm sorry to have to resort to capital letters, but what is wrong with you people?

Which brings me to the point of this: the egg-white omelette. I have friends who eat egg-white omelettes. Every time I'm forced to watch them eat egg-white omelettes, I feel bad for them. In the first place, egg-white omelettes are tasteless. In the second place, the people who eat them think they are doing something virtuous when they are instead merely misinformed. Sometimes I try to explain that what they're doing makes no sense, but they pay no attention to me because they have all been told to avoid dietary cholesterol by their doctors. According to **The New York Times**, the doctors are not deliberately misinforming their patients; instead, they're the victims of something known as the informational cascade, which turns out to be something that's repeated so many times that it becomes true even though it isn't. (Why isn't it called the misinformational cascade, I wonder.) In any case, the true victims of this misinformation are not the doctors but the people I know who've been brainwashed into thinking that egg-white omelettes are good for you.

So this is my moment to say what's been in my heart for years: it's time to put a halt to the egg-white omelette. I don't want to confuse this with something actually important, like the war in Afghanistan, which it's also time to put a halt to, but I don't seem be able to do anything about the war, whereas I have a shot at cutting down consumption of egg-white omelettes, especially with the wind of this new book in my sails.

You don't make an omelette by taking out the yolks. You make one by putting additional yolks in. A really great omelette has two whole eggs and one extra yolk, and by the way, the same thing goes for scrambled eggs. As for egg salad, here's our recipe: boil eighteen eggs, peel them, and send six of the egg whites to friends in California who persist in thinking that egg whites matter in any way. Chop the remaining twelve eggs and six yolks coarsely with a knife, and add Hellmann's mayonnaise and salt and pepper to taste.

I Just Want to Say: Teflon

I feel bad about Teflon.

It was great while it lasted.

Now it turns out to be bad for you.

Or, to put it more exactly, now it turns out that a chemical that's released when you heat up Teflon gets into your bloodstream and probably causes cancer and birth defects.

I loved Teflon. I loved the no-carb ricotta pancake I invented last year, which can be cooked only on Teflon. I loved my Silverstone Teflon-coated frying pan, which makes a beautiful steak. I loved Teflon as an adjective; it gave us a Teflon president (Ronald Reagan) and it even gave us a Teflon Don (John Gotti), whose Teflonness eventually wore out, making him an almost exact metaphorical duplicate of my Teflon pans. I loved the fact that Teflon was invented by someone named Roy J. Plunkett, whose name alone should have ensured Teflon against ever becoming a dangerous product.

But recently DuPont, the manufacturer of poly-tetrafluoroethylene (PTFE) resin, which is what Teflon was called when it first popped up as a laboratory accident back in 1938, reached a $16.5 million settlement with the Environmental Protection Agency; it seems the company knew all along that Teflon was bad for you. It's an American cliché by now: a publicly traded company holds the patent on a scientific breakthrough, it turns out to cause medical problems, and the company knew all along. You can go to the bank on it.

But it's sad about Teflon.

When it first came onto the market, Teflon wasn't good. The pans were light and skimpy and didn't compare to copper or cast iron. They were great for omelettes, and, of course, nothing stuck to them, but they were nowhere near as good for cooking things that were meant to be browned, like steaks. But then manufacturers like Silverstone produced

I Just Want to Say: Teflon

Teflon pans that were heavy-duty, and you could produce a steak that was as dark and delicious as one made on the barbecue. Unfortunately, this involved heating your Teflon pan up to a very high temperature before adding the steak, which happens to be the very way perfluoroctanoic acid (PFOA) is released into the environment. PFOA is the bad guy here, and DuPont has promised to eliminate it from all Teflon products by 2015. I'm sure that will be a comfort to those of you under the age of forty, but to me it simply means that my last years on this planet will be spent, at least in part, scraping debris off my non-Teflon frying pans.

Rumors about Teflon have been circulating for a long time, but I couldn't help hoping they were going to turn out like the rumors about aluminum, which people thought (for a while, back in the nineties) caused Alzheimer's. That was a bad moment, since never mind giving up aluminum pots and pans, it would also have meant giving up aluminum foil, disposable aluminum baking pans, and, most crucial of all, antiperspirants. I rode out that rumor, and I'm pleased to report that it went away.

But this rumor is clearly for real, so I suppose I am going to have to throw away my Teflon pans.

Meanwhile, I am going to make one last ricotta pancake breakfast:

75

Beat one egg, add one-third cup fresh whole-milk ricotta, and whisk together. Heat up a Teflon pan until carcinogenic gas is released into the air. Spoon tablespoons of batter into the frying pan and cook about two minutes on one side, until brown. Carefully flip. Cook for another minute to brown the other side. Eat with jam, if you don't care about carbs, or just eat unadorned. Serves one.

I Just Want to Say:
No, I Do Not Want Another
Bottle of Pellegrino

We would like a bottle of Pellegrino. The waiter brings the Pellegrino. There are four of us at the table. The waiter brings glasses for the Pellegrino. The glasses happen to be extremely tall. Tall glasses are not necessarily the best glasses for Pellegrino, but before I can say a word on this profound subject, the waiter pours the Pellegrino into the tall glasses.

When the waiter is done pouring, there's a tiny amount of Pellegrino left in the bottle. My husband takes a sip of his Pellegrino, and the waiter is back, in a flash, with the last drops of our Pellegrino. He tops off my husband's drink.

The first bottle of Pellegrino is now gone. We've been at the table for exactly three minutes and somehow we've managed to empty an entire bottle of Pellegrino.

"Would you like another bottle of Pellegrino?" the waiter says.

I haven't even had any of this one!

I don't actually say these words.

I love salt. I absolutely adore it. Occasionally I eat at a place where (in my opinion) the food doesn't need more salt, but it's rare.

Many years ago, they used to put salt and pepper on the table in a restaurant, and here's how they did it: there was a saltshaker and there was a pepper shaker. The pepper shaker contained ground black pepper, which was outlawed in the 1960s and replaced by the Permanent Floating Pepper Mill and the Permanent Floating Pepper Mill refrain: "Would you like some fresh ground black pepper on your salad?" I've noticed that almost no one wants some fresh ground black pepper on his salad. Why they even bother asking is a mystery to me.

But I wasn't talking about pepper, I was talking about salt. And as I was saying, there always used to be salt on the table. Now, half the time, there's none.

No, I Do Not Want Another Bottle of Pellegrino

The reason there's no salt is that the chef is forcefully trying to convey that the food has already been properly seasoned and therefore doesn't need more salt. I resent this deeply. I resent that asking for salt makes me seem aggressive toward the chef, when in fact it's the other way around. As for the other half of the time—when there **is** salt on the table—it's not what I consider salt. It's what's known as sea salt. (Sea salt used to be known as kosher salt, but that's not an upscale enough name for it anymore.) Sea salt comes in an itty-bitty dish. You always spill it trying to move it from the dish to the food on your plate, but that's the least of it: it doesn't really function as salt. It doesn't dissolve and make your food taste saltier; instead, it sits like little hard pebbles on top of it. Also, it scratches your tongue.

"Is everything all right?"
The main course has been served, and the waiter has just asked us this question. I've had exactly one bite of my main course, which is just enough for me to remember that, as usual, the main course always disappoints. I am beginning to wonder whether this is a metaphor, and if so, whether it's worth dwelling on. Now the waiter has appeared, pepper mill in one hand, Pellegrino in the other, and interrupted an extremely good story right before the punch line to ask if everything is all right.

The answer is no, it's not.

Actually the answer is, No, it's not! You ruined the punch line! Go away!

I don't say this either.

We have ordered dessert. They are giving us dessert spoons. Dessert spoons are large, oval-shaped spoons. They are so large that you could go for a swim in them. I'm not one of those people who likes to blame the French for things, especially since the French turned out to be so very very right about Iraq, but there's no question this trend began in France, where they've always had a weakness for dessert spoons.

One of the greatest things about this land of ours, as far as I'm concerned, was that we never fell into the dessert-spoon trap. If you needed a spoon for dessert, you were given a teaspoon. But those days are over, and it's a shame.

Here's the thing about dessert—you want it to last. You want to savor it. Dessert is so delicious. It's so sweet. It's so bad for you so much of the time. And, as with all bad things, you want it to last as long as possible. But you can't make it last if they give you a great big spoon to eat it with. You'll gobble up your dessert in two big gulps. Then it will be gone. And the meal will be over.

Why don't they get this? It's so obvious.

It's so obvious.

I Just Want to Say:
The World Is Not Flat

Last week I went to one of those Internet conferences I get invited to now and then, and of course **New York Times** columnist Thomas Friedman was there. He wasn't actually there in person. It wasn't that important a conference. He sent a tape of himself. He took the entire thesis of his best-selling book **The World Is Flat** and squished it down into twenty minutes. Coincidentally, two nights earlier, I had found myself standing across from Friedman, in person, at a craps table in Las Vegas. As he rolled the dice to make a five, I shouted, "This is it, Tom, this is your chance to make up for being wrong on Iraq." But he rolled a seven and crapped out.

And then there he was at this conference. There was a big banner over the screen that said THE WORLD IS FLAT, and all the bright, young Internet people watched Friedman talk about globalization and say that technology had flattened the walls of the world. They were enthralled by him and actually managed to stay focused and off their mobile devices for the entire time he was speaking. Afterward, instantly, they all turned their mobile devices back on, and the huge conference room was suddenly illuminated by hundreds of small boxes and orchestrated by the sound of thousands of tiny fingers tapping away.

Friedman, of course, is not just a columnist for the world's most powerful newspaper—he's something else. He's a panelist. There's an entire population of panelists today, mostly guys, who make a living in some way or another but whose true career consists of appearing at conferences like this. Some of these panelists are players and some are merely journalists, but for a brief moment, the panel equalizes them all. The panelists perform in front of audiences that include ordinary people, but their real performances are for one another at places like the Foursquare Conference in New York and Herbert

Allen's summer CEO-fest in Sun Valley; the panelists' job is to put into perspective whatever conventional wisdom happens to apply at the moment, and to validate it.

In fact, these conferences tend to be validating in every way, and it's no surprise that at the last two I attended, there were representatives from Walmart who appeared onstage and were never once asked about their public-relations difficulties over pesky things like the way they treat their employees. (At both conferences, though, the men from Walmart were cheerfully asked about their company's policy of requiring executives to fly tourist and sleep two-in-a-room on business trips. Both times the men from Walmart cheerfully replied. Both times the audience cheerfully chuckled along.)

Anyway, it interests me that every time I go to one of these conferences, there's a piece of absolutely unarguable conventional wisdom about the Internet that seems sooner or later to turn out to be wrong. It's not easy to be wrong about the Internet—the Internet consists of pretty much everything in the universe. So pretty much anything you say about it is going to turn out to be partly true in some way or other. Nonetheless, it turns out not to be.

For example, when I started going to these conferences, it was a given that the Internet was going to set everyone free; this was back in the day, when we understood the Internet to mean e-mail. The world was full of executives and panelists who took the position that it was much simpler to return twenty e-mails than ten telephone calls. But executives now return hundreds of e-mails every day, and life is not remotely simpler. They return e-mails day and night. They never go home from their e-mail. What's more, they absorb almost nothing that happens, because the minute it does, their BlackBerrys are blinking at them.

Then the dot-com boom began, and a new piece of conventional wisdom emerged: the dot-coms would make us rich. This was true. They did. And then, suddenly, the dot-coms crashed. So not quite true.

Time for a new piece of conventional wisdom: there was no money in the Internet. This was confounding: it seemed that an amazing, unheard-of, completely mystifying episode had occurred in the history of capitalism. A huge business had emerged, but there was no profit in it. Warren Buffett, who is the king of the panelists, the überpanelist, the second-richest man in America, the sage of Omaha who plays online bridge with the first-richest man in America, gave a speech during this period, and reminded all his acolytes that between 1904 and 1908 there were 240 automobile companies in business; by 1924, 10 of them accounted for 90 percent of revenues. This sentence was quoted as if it had come straight from the Mount, although no one was entirely sure what it meant. Was everyone going to go out of business, or just almost everyone? The guys who'd started in garages would make money, of course—they'd already made money. The guys who'd invented the technology and the software would be rich. But everyone who'd come afterward would be doomed.

Many panels were held on this point, and many panelists were thoughtful and interesting (and puzzled) about the bleak future ahead. But one thing was clear: there was no money in the Internet. And advertising was not the answer: advertising would never work because the people using the Internet would never ever accept it. The Internet was free. The Internet was democratic. The Internet was pure. Ads would never fly. What's more, in the TiVo world we now live in, the ads would be blocked by Internet users who would never stand for them.

Which brings me to this conference on the Internet I attended last week, where, it will not surprise you to hear, there was a new piece of conventional wisdom: there were billions of dollars to be made in the Internet. It had suddenly become clear that there was a lot of advertising money out there, and all you had to do was provide content so that the ads had something to run alongside of. It crossed my mind that the actual definition of "content" for an Internet company was "something you can run an ad alongside of." I found this a depressing insight, even though my conviction that all conventional wisdom about the Internet turns out to be untrue rescued me somewhat from a slough of despond on the subject.

And by the way, the world is not flat. There are walls everywhere. If there weren't, we wouldn't have gone into Iraq, where everybody crapped out, not just Tom Friedman.

I Just Want to Say:
Chicken Soup

The other day I felt a cold coming on. So I decided to have chicken soup to ward off the cold. Nevertheless, I got the cold. This happens all the time: you think you're getting a cold; you have chicken soup; you get the cold anyway. So is it possible that chicken soup gives you a cold?

Pentimento

I met Lillian Hellman just before her memoir **Penti-mento** was published in 1973. I was working as an editor at **Esquire** and we were publishing two sections from the book, one of them called "Turtle." It was about Hellman and Dashiell Hammett. I'd never seen any of Lillian Hellman's plays, and I'd struggled with Hammett's mysteries, but I read "Turtle" in galleys before we printed it, and I thought it was the most romantic thing ever written. It's a story about a vicious snapping turtle that

Hellman and Hammett kill. They slice its head off and leave it in the kitchen to be made into soup. It somehow resurrects itself, crawls out the door, and dies in the woods, prompting a long, elliptical, cut-throat debate between Hammett and Hellman about whether the turtle is some sort of amphibious reincarnation of Jesus.

I have no excuse for my infatuation with this story. I was not stupid, and I was not particularly young, both of which might be exculpatory. Like many people who read **Pentimento**, it never crossed my mind that the stories in it were fiction, and the dialogue an inadvertent parody of Hammett's tough-guy style. I thought it was divine. I immediately called **The New York Times Book Review** and asked if I could interview Hellman on the occasion of **Pentimento**'s publication. They said yes.

Hellman was already on her way to her remarkable third act. She'd published **An Unfinished Woman**, a memoir, which had been a best seller and National Book Award winner, and now with **Pentimento** she was on the verge of an even bigger best seller. She turned up on talk shows and charmed the hosts as she puffed on her cigarettes and blew smoke. With her two successful books, she'd eradicated the memory of her last few plays, which had been failures. Eventually the most famous story from **Pentimento**, "Julia," was made into a movie, with Jane Fonda as Lillian Hellman, Jason Robards as Hammett, and Vanessa Redgrave as Julia, the brave anti-Nazi spy whom Hellman claimed she'd smuggled $50,000 to in Germany in 1939, in a fur hat. The end of Hellman's life was a train wreck, but that came later. I wrote a play about it, but that came even later.

Lillian was sixty-eight when I met her, and by any standard, even of the times, she looked at least ten years older. She had never been a beauty, but once she'd been young; now she was wrinkled and close to blind. She had a whiskey voice. She used a cigarette holder and one of those ashtrays that look like beanbags, with a little metal contraption in the middle for snuffing out the ash. Because she could barely see, the question of whether the perilously ever-lengthening ash would ever make it to the ash-tray without landing in her lap and setting her on fire provided added suspense to every minute spent with her.

But in some strange way that you will have to take my word for, she was enormously attractive—vibrant, flirtatious, and intimate.

I went to see her at her home on Martha's Vineyard, which sat on a rocky beach near Chilmark. The interview is an embarrassment. I did not ask a tough question, and, by the way, I didn't have one. I was besotted. She was the woman who had said to the House Un-American Activities Committee: "I cannot cut my conscience to fit this year's patterns." She had loved the toughest guy there was, and although he had been drunk for almost their entire time together, he loved her back. Now it turned out she had practically stopped Hitler.

In the afternoon after our first interview, I went for a walk down to Lillian's beach. I'd been there no more than a few minutes when a man turned up. I had no idea where he'd come from. He was older, gray-haired, fleshy. He asked if I was staying with Lillian. I immediately became nervous. I stood up and made some sort of excuse and walked as quickly as I could over the rocks and back to the house. Lillian was sitting out on the patio in a muumuu.

"How was the beach?" she asked.

"Fine," I said.

"Was anyone else there?"

"A man," I said.

"Older?" she said. "Fat?"

"Yes," I said.

"That does it," she said.

She stood up and took off toward the beach.

A few minutes later she came back. The intruder had vanished. She was in a rage. She was apparently in an ongoing war with the man. Goddamn it, she'd told him to stay off her beach. Goddamn it, she'd told him to stop trying to have conversations with her friends. She would tell him again, if he ever dared to come around and she caught him lurking there. She was furious that he'd disappeared before she'd had the chance to order him away. I couldn't believe it. She was dying for a fight. She loved confrontation. She was a dramatist and she needed drama. I was a journalist and I liked to watch. I was in awe.

After my very bad interview with her appeared in **The Times,** Lillian and I became friends. "Friends" is probably not the right word—I became one of the young people in her life. She wrote me letters all the time, funny letters, mostly typed, and signed Miss Hellman. She sent me recipes. She came to my apartment and I went to hers. It was hard to imagine Lillian had ever been a Communist, I have to say that. I'd grown up knowing a lot of left-wing people in Hollywood who lived well, but there was no trace of the Old Left in Lillian's apartment at 630 Park Avenue—no Mexican art, for instance, or Ben Shahns; it was furnished in a style that fell somewhere between old WASP and German Jewish—brocade sofas, small tables made of dark wood, oil paintings of the sea, Persian rugs.

She held small dinners for six or eight, and she always had rollicking stories to tell that I now realize were exaggerated, but which at the time were hilarious. She'd had a run-in with a saleswoman one Sunday in the fur department of Bergdorf Goodman. Jason Epstein had set her kitchen on fire making Chinese food. Lillian was fun. She was so much fun. She had a great deep laugh, and she always had a subject for general conversation. "My great-uncle has died," she said one night at her table, "and the lawyer called to say, 'He has left you a pleasant sum of money.' How much money do you think is a pleasant sum of money?" What a game! What a wonderful game! We eventually agreed, after much debate, that $675,000 was our idea of a pleasant sum of money. She said we had guessed it on the nose. Was it true? Was any of it true? Who knows? I listened, enthralled, as she told me how Hammett had once run off with S. J. Perelman's wife, how Peter Feibleman (to whom she eventually left her home on the Vineyard) had hurt her feelings by trying to make a date with one of her good friends, how she'd once seen a young woman she thought might be Julia's daughter. This last episode took place on a cliff, as I recall. Lillian and Dashiell Hammett had been standing on a cliff when a young woman came up to her, touched her arm, and ran away. "I've always wondered," she said. "Because she looked so much like Julia."

Here is a letter she wrote me about delicatessens, my father, Henry Ephron, and me:

I am sitting in P. J. Bernstein's Delicatessen,
a place I visit about once a month. I have long been sentimental about middle-aged ladies who have to use their legs and several of the waitresses, being Jewish, have pounded on this unspoken sympathy. One of them knows that I do something, but she does not know exactly what I do; that doesn't stop her from kissing me as I order my knockwurst.

A few days ago, when she finished with the kissing, she said, "You know Henry Aarons?" "No," I said, "I don't." She pushed me with that Jewish shoulder-breaking shove. "Sure you do," she said, "his daughter." "Maybe," I said, my shoulder alive. When she returned with the knockwurst, she said, "His daughter, some fine writer, eh?" I said I didn't know, my shoulder now healed. She said, "What kind of talk is that? You don't know a fine writer when you hear a fine writer?" "Where does Mr. Aarons live?" I said, hoping to get things going in a better direction. "Do I go there?" She said, "He comes here." Well, in the next twenty minutes, by the time I had indigestion, it turned out it was your father she was talking about who, by coincidence, two hours later, called me to say that he had seen Julia.

I don't know why I tell you this, but somewhere, of course, I must wish to make you feel guilty.

It's a delightful letter, isn't it? I have a pile of her letters. When I look through them, it all comes back to me—how much I'd loved the early letters, how charmed I'd been, how flattered, how much less charming they began to seem, how burdensome they became, and then, finally, how boring.

The story of love.

Here was a thing Lillian liked to do: the T.L. Most people nowadays don't know what a T.L. is, but my mother had taught us the expression, although I can't imagine why.

T.L. stands for Trade Last, and here's how it works: you call someone up and tell her you have a T.L. for her. This means you've heard a compliment about her—and you will repeat it—but only if she first tells you a compliment someone has said about you. In other words, you will pass along a compliment, but only if you trade it last.

This, needless to say, is a strange, ungenerous, and seriously narcissistic way to tell someone a nice thing that has been said about them.

"Miss Ephron," she would say when she called, "it's Miss Hellman. I have a T.L. for you."

The first few times this happened, I was happy to play—the air was full of nice things about Lillian. She was the girl of the year. But as time passed, the calls became practically nightmarish. Everything was starting to catch up with her. She'd written another book, **Scoundrel Time**, a self-aggrandizing work about her decision not to testify before HUAC, and followed it with her somewhat problematical decision to pose for a Blackglama mink ad. People were talking about her, but not in any way that gave me something to trade. Not that I was hearing much of it—I was living in Washington, and people in Washington don't talk about anyone who doesn't live in Washington, and that's the truth.

But there she was, on the other end of phone, waiting for me to come up with my end of the T.L. My brain would desperately race trying to think of something I could say, anything. I had to be careful, because I didn't want to get caught in a lie. And if I made up a story, I had to be sure I was quoting a man, because despite her warmth to me, Lillian didn't care about nice things women said about her. And I couldn't say, "I'm in Washington, no one here is talking about you." So I would eventually make something up, usually about how much my husband adored her (which was true). But it never really satisfied her. Because what Lillian really wanted to hear, T.L.-wise, was that I'd just spent the evening with someone like Robert Redford (to pick an imaginary episode out of the air) and that he'd confessed that he desperately wanted to sleep with her.

When my marriage ended and I moved back to New York, Lillian was shocked. She couldn't imagine why I'd left him. She called and asked me to reconsider. She said I ought to forgive him.

Neither my husband nor I had the remotest interest in our getting back together, but Lillian was determined, and she kept pressing me. Can't you forgive him? I took the moment to slip out of her life.

I told myself that I could never have gone on with the friendship because of the way Lillian had reacted to the divorce.

Then, about a year later, a woman named Muriel Gardiner wrote a book about her life as a spy before World War II, and it became clear that Hellman had stolen her story. There was no Julia, and Lillian had never saved Europe with her little fur hat.

I told myself I could never have gone on with the friendship because Lillian had turned out to be a pathological liar.

Then Lillian sued Mary McCarthy for calling her a liar.

And I told myself I could never have gone on with the friendship because I could never respect someone who had turned against the First Amendment.

I actually did. I actually told myself that.

But the truth is that any excuse will do when this sort of romance comes to an end. The details are just details. And the story is always the same: the younger woman idolizes the older woman; she stalks her; the older woman takes her up; the younger woman finds out the older woman is only human; the story ends.

If the younger woman is a writer, she eventually writes something about the older woman.

And then years pass.

And she herself gets older.

And there are moments when she would like to apologize—at least for the way it ended.

And this may be one of them.

My Life as a Meat Loaf

A while back, my friend Graydon Carter mentioned that he was opening a restaurant in New York. I cautioned him against this, because it's my theory that owning a restaurant is the kind of universal fantasy everyone ought to grow out of, sooner rather than later, or else you will be stuck with the restaurant. There are many problems that come with owning a restaurant, not the least of which is that you have to eat there all the time. Giving up the fantasy that you want to own a restaurant is probably the last Piaget stage.

But Graydon cheerfully persisted, and the restaurant he opened downtown became a huge success. A year later, he told me he was going to open a second restaurant, this one uptown, in the old location of the Monkey Bar. He said he hoped it would be something like the Ivy in London, which is one of my favorite places, and did I have any suggestions for the menu? I immediately sent a long list. At the top of it was meat loaf. I love meat loaf. It feels like home.

A few months before the restaurant opened, I was invited to a tasting. It included an unusual dish consisting of two thick slabs of meat loaf that had been sautéed slightly and were firm on the outside. This made for a nice combination of squishy and crispy and thus avoided the primary pitfall of meat loaf, which is that it's so soft and mushy you can polish it off in under a minute. I would not say that this particular meat loaf felt like home exactly, but it was delicious nonetheless. It came covered with a lovely mushroom sauce, which made sense given the crisp exterior. Normally I would take a strong position against mushroom sauce, but this meat loaf seemed to cry out for it, and not in a bad way.

I had no idea the Monkey Bar meat loaf was going to have my name on it, but when the restaurant opened, there it was, on the menu, Nora's Meat Loaf. I felt that I had to order it, out of loyalty to myself, and it was exactly as good as it had been at the tasting. I was delighted. What's more, I had the oddest sense of accomplishment. I somehow felt I'd created this meat loaf, even though I'd had nothing to do with it. I'd always envied Nellie Melba for her peach, Princess Margherita for her pizza, and Reuben for his sandwich, and now I was sort of one of them. Nora's Meat Loaf. It was something to remember me by. It wasn't exactly what I was thinking of back in the day when we used to play a game called "If you could have something named after you, what would it be?" In that period, I'd hoped for a dance step, or a pair of pants. But I was older now, and I was willing to settle for a meat loaf.

By the way, I was not the only person whose name was on the Monkey Bar menu. My friend Louise had a salad named after her. It's called Louise's Sunset Salad.

In the next couple of weeks, I got five or six e-mails from friends complimenting me on "my" meat loaf.

Here's what I did not say in reply:
1. I had nothing to do with it.
2. It's not really my meat loaf.
3. My meat loaf has a package of Lipton onion soup mix in it and this one doesn't.

I said instead:
1. Thank you.
2. I'm so glad you ordered it.
3. It **is** good, isn't it.

I was proud. My meat loaf was a huge hit. It was out there working for me, even though I was not: I was just sitting home surfing the Net and wasting entire days thinking about what to do about the living room.

The next time I went to the Monkey Bar, I ordered the meat loaf again. After all, if I wasn't ordering the meat loaf, how could I expect anyone else to? But, alarmingly, something had happened to it. Instead of two slabs of meat loaf, there was now just one, and the mushroom sauce was being served on the side. I entered into a conversation about this development with the maître d', who listened politely and then explained that another customer had suggested that the mushroom sauce be put on the side, so now it was being put on the side. I couldn't help thinking that I might have been consulted about this change. I gently suggested that a fairly calamitous mistake had been made. I said I was the queen of On the Side, but that this meat loaf was begging for the mushroom sauce to be served right on top of it. The maître d' promised to think about it.

A couple of weeks passed and I noticed, suddenly, that, like the dogs that did not bark in **The Hound of the Baskervilles**, I had not received any e-mails lately complimenting me on "my" meat loaf. The next time I went to the Monkey Bar, my friend

Alessandra was there. After dinner she came over to our table and said, "The meat loaf tastes like a hockey puck."

I was stunned. I knew the meat loaf was deteriorating, but a hockey puck? I wondered about our friendship. Had Alessandra not noticed my name was on the meat loaf? What if it were truly my meat loaf instead of one that my name had been frivolously attached to without even asking me? It seemed cruel and insensitive on her part.

That was on a Saturday night. On Monday I got an e-mail from my friend Sandy. It said: "Re: Monkey Bar meat loaf. Sue them."

So I wrote an e-mail to Graydon, quite a long thing saying that while I did not mean to make trouble, I was compelled to tell him that people were talking about the meat loaf, and what they were saying wasn't good. He e-mailed back to say that they were way ahead of me—they'd just fired the chef and replaced him with the famous Larry Forgione. They'd been unhappy for weeks. The meat loaf was only a symptom.

So Larry Forgione came in and changed the menu and the recipe for the meat loaf. It became a traditional meat loaf, tasty and moist, and while it didn't seem to have a package of Lipton onion soup mix in it, it truly tasted like home. The mushroom sauce was still there, kind of swirling around on the plate, I don't know why, because this meat loaf didn't really call for it. But there it was, the food equivalent of a vestigial tail.

I was relieved. I could relax. My meat loaf had been saved, and now I could order some of the other things on the Monkey Bar menu. One of them was a perfect version of Chasen's chili, served with a corn muffin. It was so heavenly that I decided to be faithful to it for a while. Eventually I noticed that the meat loaf had been downgraded slightly to a Tuesday night special, but I was too busy practicing monogamy with the chili to worry about the meat loaf.

I am writing this because yesterday I went to the Monkey Bar. It was a Tuesday. On the way there, I thought I might check up on my meat loaf. I opened the menu, and before I read a word I somehow knew what I was going to see—or rather, what I was not going to see.

My meat loaf was gone.

Louise's Sunset Salad was still on the regular menu, but Nora's Meat Loaf was gone.

It had bombed. There was no other way to look at it.

I asked if anyone had mentioned it now that it was gone. I asked if anyone had complained. I asked if anyone had even noticed. No one has. It's as if it never even happened.

My Life as a Meat Loaf

It's been replaced as the Tuesday special by spaghetti and meatballs. I ordered it, hoping to discover that a grave injustice had been done, but the spaghetti and meatballs were excellent. I made a small suggestion about the consistency of the grated Parmesan cheese that's served with them, and I just hope someone listens to me.

Addicted to L-U-V

A few years ago, I stumbled onto something called Scrabble Blitz. It was a four-minute version of Scrabble solitaire, on a Web site called Games.com, and I began playing it without a clue that within one day—I am not exaggerating—it would fry my brain. I'm no stranger to this sort of thing: one summer when I was young, I became so addicted to croquet that I had a series of recurrent dreams in which I was holding a croquet mallet and whacking my mother's head through a wicket.

The same sort of thing happened with Scrabble Blitz, although my mother, who has been dead for many years, was left out of it. I began having Scrabble dreams in which people turned into letter tiles that danced madly about. I tuned out on conversations and instead thought about how many letters there were in the name of the person I wasn't listening to. I fell asleep memorizing the two- and three-letter words that distinguish those of us who are hooked on Scrabble from those of you who aren't. (For instance, while you were not paying attention to Scrabble, the following have become words in the Scrabble dictionary: "qi," "za," and "ka." Don't ask me what they mean, but my guess is that in the tradition of all such things, they are Indonesian coins. "Luv" is also a word, by the way, as is "suq.")

Remember that ad, "This is your brain. This is your brain on drugs"? That was me. My brain turned to cheese. I could feel it happening. It was clear that I was becoming more and more scattered, more distracted, more unfocused: I was exhibiting all the symptoms of terminal ADD; I was turning into a teenage boy. I instantly became an expert on how the Internet could alter your brain in a permanent way, and I offered my opinions on this subject at all sorts of places, where, as I recall, no one was particularly interested.

The Scrabble Blitz site was full of other deranged

Scrabble Blitzers, who dealt with their addiction by writing comments about it in the Web site chat room during the two-minute break between games, the two-minute break being a perfect time to log off and stop playing Scrabble Blitz but you didn't because you were totally hooked and besides you were going to play only one more game, or maybe two. The comments consisted of things like: "I'm an addict, lol" and "I can't stop playing this ha ha." My contempt for these comments led me to think I was somehow different from the people who wrote them, but the truth is I wasn't—I was exactly like them except for the lol's and the ha ha's, and even I have used an lol and a ha ha from time to time, though not in a chat room, and most of the time, I hope, ironically, but to be perfectly honest, not every time.

The game of Scrabble Blitz eventually became too much for the Web site. Lag was a huge problem. From time to time, the Scrabble Blitz area would shut down for days, and when it returned, so did all the addicts, full of comments about how they had barely withstood life without the game. I began to get carpal tunnel syndrome from playing—I'm not kidding. I realized I was going to have to kick the habit. I thought about kicking the habit. I promised myself I would. After one more game. After one more day. After one more week. And then, one day, out of the blue, I was saved by what's known in the insurance business as an act of God: Games.com shut down Scrabble Blitz permanently. And that was that. It was gone.

I went back to online Scrabble, a mild and soporific version of the game. I restricted myself to two games a day—no more. I spent several years wandering from one Scrabble Web site to another—there are several—and recently found my way to a place called Scrabulous.com. I've been playing on this Web site for just over fifty days—I know because I recently received a congratulatory e-mail from "The Scrabulous Team" on the occasion of my one hundredth game. It crossed my mind when I got the e-mail that even two games a day was too much. But it didn't stop me from playing: my habit was under control.

But this week, I had a major setback. I went onto the Scrabulous site to play my customary two games, and to my amazement, right there on the entry page, was a chance to play Scrabble Blitz. Only it wasn't called Scrabble Blitz. It was called Blitz Scrabble. It was back. It was working perfectly. And not only was it back, so were all the people I used to play with, all of them making their sad little jokes about being addicted to the game, followed by lol or ha ha and even an occasional ☺. I decided to play just one game, or maybe two. An hour later, I was still there. My heart was racing. My brain was once again turning to cheese. I was hooked.

It's now been five days—five days when I've either been playing Blitz Scrabble or thinking about playing Blitz Scrabble. Five days while tiles danced through my head as I fell asleep. Five days of turning into a teenage boy once again. It's quite clear that there's only one solution: I am going to have to go to the Parental Controls dial on my computer—I'm sure there is one—and put Scrabulous.com on the Don't Go There list, or whatever it's called.

So good-bye. I'm going. I am definitely going.

But first, I'm going to play my last game of Blitz Scrabble. Make that my second-to-last. Or third. ☺

The Six Stages of E-Mail

Stage One: Infatuation

I just got e-mail! I can't believe it! It's so great! Here's my handle. Write me. Who said letter-writing was dead? Were they ever wrong. I'm writing letters like crazy for the first time in years. I come home and ignore all my loved ones and go straight to the computer to make contact with total strangers. And how great is AOL? It's so easy. It's so friendly. It's a community. Wheeeee! I've got mail!

Stage Two: Clarification

Okay, I'm starting to understand—e-mail isn't letter-writing at all, it's something else entirely. It was just invented, it was just born, and overnight it turns out to have a form and a set of rules and a language all its own. Not since the printing press. Not since television. It's revolutionary. It's life-altering. It's shorthand. Cut to the chase. Get to the point. It saves so much time. It takes five seconds to accomplish in an e-mail something that takes five minutes on the telephone. The phone requires you to converse, to say things like hello and good-bye, to pretend to some semblance of interest in the person on the other end of the line. Worst of all, the phone occasionally forces you to make actual plans with the people you talk to—to suggest lunch or dinner—even if you have no desire whatsoever to see them. No danger of that with e-mail. E-mail is a whole new way of being friends with people: intimate but not, chatty but not, communicative but not; in short, friends but not. What a breakthrough. How did we ever live without it? I have more to say on this subject, but I have to answer an instant message from someone I almost know.

Stage Three: Confusion

I have done nothing to deserve any of this: Viagra!!!!!
Best Web source for Vioxx. Spend a week in Can-
cún. Have a rich beautiful lawn. Astrid would like to
be added as one of your friends. XXXXXXXVideos.
Add three inches to the length of your penis. The
Democratic National Committee needs you. Virus
Alert. FW: This will make you laugh. FW: This is
funny. FW: This is hilarious. FW: Grapes and raisins
toxic for dogs. FW: Gabriel García Márquez's Final
Farewell. FW: Kurt Vonnegut's Commencement
Address. FW: The Neiman Marcus Chocolate Chip
Cookie recipe. AOL Member: We value your opinion. A message from Barack Obama. Find low mort-
gage payments, Nora. Nora, it's your time to shine.
Need to fight off bills, Nora? Yvette would like to be
added as one of your friends. You have failed to
establish a full connection to AOL.

Stage Four: Disenchantment

Help! I'm drowning. I have 112 unanswered e-mails.
I'm a writer—imagine how many unanswered
e-mails I would have if I had a real job. Imagine how
much writing I could do if I didn't have to answer all
this e-mail. My eyes are dim. My wrist hurts. I can't

focus. Every time I start to write something, the e-mail icon starts bobbing up and down and I'm compelled to check whether anything good or interesting has arrived. It hasn't. Still, it might, any second now. And yes, it's true—I can do in a few seconds with e-mail what would take much longer on the phone, but most of my e-mails are from people who don't have my phone number and would never call me in the first place. In the brief time it took me to write this paragraph, three more e-mails arrived. Now I have 115 unanswered e-mails. Strike that: 116. Glub glub glub glub glub.

Stage Five: Accommodation

Yes. No. Can't. No way. Maybe. Doubtful. Sorry. So sorry. Thanks. No thanks. Out of town. OOT. Try me in a month. Try me in the fall. Try me in a year. NoraE@aol.com can now be reached at NoraE81082@gmail.com.

Stage Six: Death

Call me.

Flops

I have had a lot of flops.

I have had movies that were total flops.

When I say total flops, I mean they got bad reviews and they didn't make money.

I have also had partial flops: they got good reviews and they didn't make money.

I have also had hits.

It's lovely to have a hit. There's nothing like a hit.

But it's horrible to have a flop. It's painful and mortifying. It's lonely and sad.

A couple of my flops eventually became cult hits, which is your last and final hope for a flop, but most of my flops remained flops.

Flops stay with you in a way that hits never do. They torture you. You toss and turn. You replay. You recast. You recut. You rewrite. You restage. You run through the what-if's and the if-only's. You cast about for blame.

One of the best things about directing movies, as opposed to merely writing them, is that there's no confusion about who's to blame: you are. But before I became a director, when I was just the screen-writer, I could cast blame everywhere. There's a movie I wrote years ago that didn't work. In my opinion. You may have seen this movie. You may even have loved it. But it was a flop when it opened; it got exactly one good review in all of America, and then it sank like a stone.

For years I tried to figure out where I'd gone wrong and what I should have done. What should I have said to the director? What should I have done in order to fight for the original draft of the script, the best draft, the one with the voice-over? What could I have done to prevent the director from inserting the fun-house sequence, or from cutting the flashbacks, which were really funny? Or were they?

I spent years wondering about all this. Then, one day, I had lunch with the movie's editor. I was about to direct my first movie, and I was looking for advice. At a certain point, we got around to the flop. He must have brought it up; I never would have. That's another thing about flops: you never talk about them afterward, they're too painful. But he assured me that nothing could have been done; the problem, he said, was the casting. This calmed me down temporarily. This was at least a solution to the riddle of why the movie hadn't worked—it was miscast. Of course. So it wasn't my fault. What a relief.

For quite a long time I comforted myself with that theory. Then, recently, I saw the movie again and I realized why the movie hadn't worked. There was nothing wrong with the cast; the problem was the script. The script wasn't good enough, it wasn't funny enough, it wasn't sharp enough. So it was my fault after all.

By the way, one of the things you hope for when your movie hasn't gotten good reviews is that some important critic will eventually embrace it and attack all the critics who didn't like when it opened. I mention this for two reasons: first, so that you'll understand how truly pathetic you become after a flop; and second, because, astonishingly, this actually happened with a movie I wrote called **Heartburn. Heartburn** flopped when it opened. A year later, Vincent Canby, the eminent movie critic for **The New York Times,** saw the movie for the first time and wrote an article calling it a small masterpiece. Those were not his exact words, but close. And he claimed to be mystified that other critics hadn't seen how good it was. But this was cold comfort, because I couldn't help wondering if things might have been different had Canby reviewed the movie in the first place. I'm not suggesting that the movie would have sold more tickets, but a good review in **The Times** cushions the blow.

One of the saddest things about a flop is that even if it turns out to have a healthy afterlife, even if it's partly redeemed, you remain bruised and hurt by the original experience. Worst of all, you eventually come to agree with the audience, the one that didn't much like it to begin with. You agree with them, even if it means you've abandoned your child.

People who aren't in the business always wonder if you knew it was going to be a flop. They say things like, "Didn't they know?" "How could they not have known?" My experience is that you don't know. You don't know because you're invested in the script. You love the cast. You adore the crew. Two or three hundred people have followed you into the wilderness; they've committed six months or a year of their lives to an endeavor you've made them believe in. It's your party, you're the host. You've fought hard to improve the on-set catering. You've flown in frozen custard from Wisconsin. And everyone is having the most wonderful time.

I now know that when you shoot a movie where the crew is absolutely hysterical with laughter and you are repeatedly told by the sound guy that you are making the funniest movie in history, you may be in trouble.

The first time this happened, I had no idea. The crew loved it. They were on the floor. The camera operator and focus puller were stuffing Kleenexes into their mouths to keep from laughing. And then we cut the movie and it tested poorly. Let me be more explicit: it tested in the way many comedies do, which is that the audience laughed at the jokes and nonetheless didn't like the movie. This is the moment when you ought to know you are approaching flop, but you don't; you think you can fix it. After all, they laughed. That must mean something. And there are so many stories about movies that were fixed after they tested badly. There is anecdotal evidence. They fixed **Fatal Attraction.** Not that your movie is remotely like **Fatal Attraction.** Still, it gives you hope.

So you recut. And you reshoot.

And it still tests poorly.

At this point, you surely know you've got a flop. You'd have to be a fool not to know.

But you don't. Because you hope. You hope against hope. You hope the critics will like it. Perhaps that will help. You hope the studio will cut a trailer for the movie that will explain the movie to the audience. You spend hours on the phone with the marketing people. You worry over the tracking figures. You pretend to yourself that test screenings don't matter—although they do, they absolutely do, especially when you make a commercial movie.

And then the movie opens and that's that. You get bad reviews and no one goes to see it. You may never work again. No one calls. No one mentions it.

But time passes. Life goes on. You're lucky enough to make another movie.

But that flop sits there, in the history of your life, like a black hole with a wildly powerful magnetic field.

By the way, there are people who have positive things to say about flops. They write books about success through failure and the power of failure. Failure, they say, is a growth experience; you learn from failure. I wish that were true. It seems to me the main thing you learn from a failure is that it's entirely possible you will have another failure.

My biggest flop was a play I wrote. It got what are known as mixed reviews—which is to say, it got some good reviews, but not in **The New York Times.** It puttered along for a couple of months, and then it died. It lost its entire investment. It was the best thing I ever wrote, so it was a particularly heartbreaking experience. If I think about it for more than a minute, I start to cry.

Flops

Some plays flop but go on to have a life in stock and amateur productions, but not this one. No one performs it anywhere, ever.

You'd think I would have given up hoping that anything good would ever happen to this play, but I haven't: I sometimes fantasize that when I'm dying, someone who's in a position to revive it will come to my bedside to say good-bye, and I will say, "Could I ask a favor?" He will say yes. What else can he say? After all, I'm dying. And I will say, "Could you please do a revival of my play?"

How pathetic is that?

Christmas Dinner

We have a traditional Christmas dinner. We've been doing it for twenty-two years. There are fourteen people involved—eight parents and six children—and we all get together at Jim and Phoebe's during Christmas week. For one night a year, we're a family, a cheerful, makeshift family, a family of friends. We exchange modest presents, we make predictions about events in the coming year, and we eat.

Each of us brings part of the dinner. Maggie brings the hors d'oeuvres. Like all people assigned to bring hors d'oeuvres, Maggie is not really into cooking, but she happens to be an exceptional purchaser of hors d'oeuvres. Jim and Phoebe do the main course because the dinner is at their house. This year they're cooking a turkey. Ruthie and I were always in charge of desserts. Ruthie's specialty was a wonderful bread pudding. I can never settle on just one dessert, so I often make three—something chocolate (like a chocolate cream pie), a fruit pie (like a tarte tatin), and a plum pudding that no one ever eats but me. I love making desserts for Christmas dinner, and I have always believed that I make excellent desserts. But now that everything has gone to hell and I've been forced to replay the last twenty-two years of Christmas dinners, I realize that the only dessert anyone ate with real enthusiasm was Ruthie's bread pudding; no one ever said anything complimentary about any of mine. How I could have sat through Christmas dinner all this time and not realized this simple truth is one of the most puzzling aspects of this story.

A little over a year ago, Ruthie died. Ruthie was my best friend. She was also Maggie's best friend and Phoebe's best friend. We were all devastated. A month after her death, we had our traditional Christmas dinner, but it wasn't the same without Ruthie—life wasn't the same, Christmas dinner wasn't the same, and Ruthie's bread pudding (which

I reproduced, from her recipe) wasn't the same either. This year, when we opened negotiations about when our Christmas dinner would take place, I told Phoebe that I'd decided I didn't want to make Ruthie's bread pudding again because it made me feel even worse about her death than I already did.

Anyway, we settled on a night for the dinner. But then Ruthie's husband, Stanley, announced that he didn't want to be there. He said he was too sad. So Phoebe decided to invite another family instead. She asked Walter and Priscilla and their kids to join us. Walter and Priscilla are good friends of ours, but four years ago Priscilla announced that she didn't like living in New York anymore and was moving, with the children, to England. Priscilla is English and therefore entitled to prefer England to New York; still, it was hard not to take it personally. But she and the kids were coming to Manhattan to join Walter for Christmas, and they accepted the invitation to our Christmas dinner. A few days later Phoebe called to tell me that she'd asked Priscilla to do one of the desserts. I was thunderstruck. I do the desserts. I love doing the desserts. I make excellent desserts. Priscilla hates doing desserts. The only dessert Priscilla ever makes is trifle, and when she serves it she always announces that she hates trifle and never eats it.

"But she will make her trifle," I said.

"She won't make her trifle," Phoebe said.

"How do you know?" I said.

"I will tell her not to make her trifle," Phoebe said. "Meanwhile, are you good at mashed potatoes?"

"Sure," I said.

"Bring mashed potatoes," Phoebe said, "because Jim and I don't have any luck with them."

"Fine," I said.

Several days passed while I thought about what desserts I would bring to Christmas dinner. I read the new Martha Stewart baking book and found a recipe for cherry pie. I went on the Internet and ordered pie cherries from Wisconsin. I bought the ingredients for the plum pudding that no one eats but me. I was thinking about making a peppermint pie. And then a shocking thing happened: Phoebe e-mailed to say that since I was doing the mashed potatoes, she'd asked Priscilla to make all the desserts. I couldn't believe it. Stripped of the desserts and downgraded to mashed potatoes? I was a legendary cook—how was this possible? It crossed my mind that Phoebe was using Ruthie's death to get me to stop making desserts. She'd probably been trying to do this for years; it was only a matter of time before I would be reassigned to hors d'oeuvres, displacing Maggie, who would doubtless be relegated to mixed nuts.

I took a bath in order to contemplate this blow to my self-image.

I got out of the bathtub and wrote an e-mail in reply to Phoebe. It said, simply, "WHAT?" I thought it was understated and brilliant and would get her attention.

Minutes later the phone rang. It was Phoebe. She wasn't calling about my e-mail at all.

"I can't believe this," she said. "I just got an e-mail from Priscilla in England saying that she's not making dessert. Instead, Walter has gone to London and bought mince pies. He's bringing them to New York. I hate mince pies. I absolutely hate them. Didn't you once make a mince pie that no one ate?"

"It was a raisin pie," I said. "And I liked it."

"Mince pies!" Phoebe said. "Who's going to eat mince pies?"

"What are you going to do?" I said.

"I've already done it," Phoebe said. "I e-mailed her back and told her the mince pies were out of the question and that she should order a Yule log and a coconut cake from Eli's and just have them delivered to me. Mince pies. Really."

"I can't believe this," I said. "I think we must be talking about the cruelest woman on the planet."

"Who?" Phoebe said.

"You," I said. "Why am I not doing the desserts? I liked doing desserts. Last year my peppermint pie was a huge hit."

"I remember that pie," Phoebe said.

"This year I ordered cherries from Wisconsin," I said. "The shipping alone cost fifty-two dollars."

"If you want to bring dessert, bring dessert," said Phoebe.

"But we don't need dessert because there are mince pies and a Yule log—"

"And a coconut cake," said Phoebe. "We've got to have a coconut cake. But you can bring anything else you want."

I hung up the phone. I was reeling. To make matters worse, I'd already gone out and bought four pints of peppermint stick ice cream for the peppermint pie I was now not going to make unless I wanted to prove that I was the all-time world champion in the can't-take-a-hint department of life. I stood there, missing Ruthie desperately. If she were alive, none of this would ever have happened. She was the glue, she was the thing that gave us the illusion that we were a family, she was the mother who loved us all so much that we loved one another, she was the spirit of Christmas. Now we were a group of raging siblings; her death had released us all to be the worst possible versions of ourselves.

I went to my computer and pulled up the pictures from the last Christmas we'd all been together. There we were, so happy, crowded together, overlapping. There was Ruthie. She had the most beautiful smile.

The next day, Walter called. He'd just arrived in New York with fourteen mince pies, and he was bringing them to Christmas dinner come hell or high water. "I love mince pie," he said. "It wouldn't be Christmas without mince pie."

I know how he feels.

Ruthie's Bread and Butter Pudding

5 large eggs
4 egg yolks
1 cup granulated sugar
¼ teaspoon salt
1 quart whole milk
1 cup heavy cream, plus 1 cup for
    serving
1 teaspoon vanilla extract
Twelve ½-inch-thick slices brioche,
    crusts removed, buttered gener-
    ously on one side
½ cup confectioners' sugar

Preheat the oven to 375 degrees. Butter a shallow two-quart baking dish.

Gently beat the eggs, egg yolks, granulated sugar, and salt until thoroughly blended.

Scald the milk and cream in a saucepan over high heat. Don't boil. When you tip the pan and the mixture spits or makes a sizzling noise, remove from the heat and stir in the vanilla extract. STIR GENTLY, don't beat, into the egg mixture until blended.

Overlap the bread, butter side up, in the prepared baking dish and pour the egg mixture over the bread. Set in a larger pan with enough hot water to come halfway up the side of the dish. Bake for about 45 minutes, or until the bread is golden-brown and a sharp knife inserted in the middle comes out clean. The bread should be golden and the pudding puffed up. This can be done early in the day. Do not chill.

Before serving, sprinkle with confectioners' sugar and place under the broiler. Don't walk away; this takes only a minute or so. Or you can use one of those crème brûlée gadgets to brown the sugar.

Serve with a pitcher of heavy cream.

The D Word

The most important thing about me, for quite a long chunk of my life, was that I was divorced. Even after I was no longer divorced but remarried, this was true. I have now been married to my third husband for more than twenty years. But when you've had children with someone you're divorced from, divorce defines everything; it's the lurking fact, a slice of anger in the pie of your brain.

Of course, there are good divorces, where everything is civil, even friendly. Child support payments arrive. Visitations take place on schedule. Your ex-husband rings the doorbell and stays on the other side of the threshold; he never walks in without knocking and helps himself to the coffee. In my next life I must get one of those divorces.

One good thing I'd like to say about divorce is that it sometimes makes it possible for you to be a much better wife to your next husband because you have a place for your anger; it's not directed at the person you're currently with.

Another good thing about divorce is that it makes clear something that marriage obscures, which is that you're on your own. There's no power struggle over which of you is going to get up in the middle of the night; you are.

But I can't think of anything good about divorce as far as the children are concerned. You can't kid yourself about that, although many people do. They say things like, It's better for children not to grow up with their parents in an unhappy marriage. But unless the parents are beating each other up, or abusing the children, kids are better off if their parents are together. Children are much too young to shuttle between houses. They're too young to handle the idea that the two people they love most in the world don't love each other anymore, if they ever did. They're too young to understand that all the wishful thinking in the world won't bring their parents back together. And the newfangled rigmarole of joint custody doesn't do any-thing to ease the cold reality: in order to see one par-ent, the divorced child must walk out on the other.

The best divorce is the kind where there are no children. That was my first divorce. You walk out the door and you never look back. There were cats, cats I was wildly attached to; my husband and I spoke in cat voices. Once the marriage was over, I never thought of the cats again (until I wrote about them in a novel and disguised them as hamsters).

A few months before my first husband and I broke up, I had a magazine assignment to write about the actors Rod Steiger and Claire Bloom and their fabu-lous marriage. I went to see them at their Fifth Avenue apartment, and they insisted on being inter-viewed separately. This should have been some sort of clue. But I was clueless. In fact, looking back, it seems to me that I was clueless until I was about fifty years old. Anyway, I interviewed the two of them in sepa-rate rooms. They seemed very happy. I wrote the piece, I turned it in, the magazine accepted it, they sent me a check, I cashed the check, and a day later, Rod Steiger and Claire Bloom announced they were getting a divorce. I couldn't believe it. Why hadn't they told me? Why had they gone forward with a magazine piece about their marriage when they were getting a divorce?

But then my own marriage ended, and about a week later a photographer turned up at my former apartment to take a picture of my husband and me for an article about our kitchen. I wasn't there, of course. I'd moved out. What's more, I'd forgotten the appointment. The reporter involved with the article was livid that I hadn't remembered, hadn't called, hadn't told her, and was no doubt angry that I'd agreed to do the interview about my marital kitchen when I had to have known I was getting a divorce. But the truth is you don't always know you're getting a divorce. For years, you're married. Then, one day, the concept of divorce enters your head. It sits there for a while. You lean toward it and then you lean away. You make lists. You calculate how much it will cost. You tote up grievances, and pluses and minuses. You have an affair. You start seeing a shrink. The two of you start seeing a shrink. And then you end the marriage, not because anything in particular happened that was worse than what had happened the day before, but simply because you suddenly have a place to stay while you look for an apartment, or $3,000 your father has unexpectedly given you.

I don't mean to leave out the context. My first marriage ended in the early 1970s, at the height of the women's movement. Jules Feiffer used to draw cartoons of young women dancing wildly around looking for themselves, and that's what we were all like. We took things way too seriously. We drew up contracts that were meant to divide the household tasks in a more equitable fashion. We joined consciousness-raising groups and sat in a circle and pretended we weren't jealous of one another. We read tracts that said the personal is political. And by the way, the personal **is** political, although not as much as we wanted to believe it was.

But the main problem with our marriages was not that our husbands wouldn't share the housework but that we were unbelievably irritable young women and our husbands irritated us unbelievably.

A thing I remember from my consciousness-raising group is that one of the women in it burst into tears one day because her husband had given her a frying pan for her birthday.

She, somehow, never got a divorce.

But the rest of us did.

We'd grown up in an era when no one was divorced, and suddenly everyone was divorced.

My second divorce was the worst kind of divorce. There were two children; one had just been born. My husband was in love with someone else. I found out about him and his affair when I was still pregnant. I had gone to New York for the day and had had a meeting with a writer-producer named Jay Presson Allen. I was about to go to LaGuardia to take the Eastern shuttle back to Washington when she handed me a script she happened to have lying around, by an English writer named Frederic Raphael. "Read this," she said. "You'll like it."

I opened it on the plane. It began with a married couple at a dinner party. I can't remember their names, but for the sake of the story, let's call them Clive and Lavinia. It was a very sophisticated dinner party and everyone at it was smart and brittle and chattering brilliantly. Clive and Lavinia were particularly clever, and they bantered with each other in a charming, flirtatious way. Everyone in the room admired them, and their marriage. The guests sat down to dinner and the patter continued. In the middle of the dinner, a man seated next to Lavinia put his hand on her leg. She put her cigarette out on his hand. The glittering conversation continued. When the dinner ended, Clive and Lavinia got into their car to drive home. The talk ceased, and they drove in absolute silence. They had nothing to say to each other. And then Lavinia said: "All right. Who is she?"

That was on page 8 of the screenplay.

I closed the script. I couldn't breathe. I knew at that moment that my husband was having an affair. I sat there, stunned, for the rest of the flight. The plane landed, and I went home and straight to his office in our apartment. There was a locked drawer. Of course. I knew there would be. I found the key. I opened the drawer and there was the evidence—a book of children's stories she'd given him, with an incredibly stupid inscription about their enduring love. I wrote about all this in a novel called **Heartburn,** and it's a very funny book, but it wasn't funny at the time. I was insane with grief. My heart was broken. I was terrified about what was going to happen to my children and me. I felt gaslighted, and idiotic, and completely mortified. I wondered if I was going to become one of those divorced women who's forced to move with her children to Connecticut and is never heard from again.

I walked out dramatically, and I came back after promises were made. My husband entered into the usual cycle for this sort of thing—lies, lies, and more lies. I myself entered into surveillance, steaming open American Express bills, swearing friends to secrecy, finding out that the friends I'd sworn to secrecy couldn't keep a secret, and so forth. There was a mysterious receipt from James Robinson Antiques. I called James Robinson and pretended to be my husband's assistant and claimed I needed to know exactly what the receipt was for so that I could insure it. The receipt turned out to be for an antique porcelain box that said "I Love You Truly" on it. It was presumably not unlike the antique porcelain box my husband had bought for me a couple of years earlier that said "Forever and Ever." I mention all this so you will understand that this is part of the process: once you find out he's cheated on you, you have to keep finding it out, over and over and over again, until you've degraded yourself so completely that there's nothing left to do but walk out.

When my second marriage ended, I was angry and hurt and shocked.

Now I think, Of course.

I think, Who can possibly be faithful when they're young?

I think, Stuff happens.

I think, People are careless and there are almost never any consequences (except for the children, which I already said).

And I survived. My religion is Get Over It. I turned it into a rollicking story. I wrote a novel. I bought a house with the money from the novel.

People always say that once it goes away, you forget the pain. It's a cliché of childbirth: you forget the pain. I don't happen to agree. I remember the pain. What you really forget is love.

Divorce seems as if it will last forever, and then suddenly, one day, your children grow up, move out, and make lives for themselves, and except for an occasional flare, you have no contact at all with your ex-husband. The divorce has lasted way longer than the marriage, but finally it's over.

Enough about that.

The point is that for a long time, the fact that I was divorced was the most important thing about me.

And now it's not.

Now the most important thing about me is that I'm old.

The O Word

I'm old.

I am sixty-nine years old.

I'm not really old, of course.

Really old is eighty.

But if you are young, you would definitely think that I'm old.

No one actually likes to admit that they're old.

The most they will cop to is that they're older. Or oldish.

In these days of physical fitness, hair dye, and

plastic surgery, you can live much of your life without feeling or even looking old.

But then one day, your knee goes, or your shoulder, or your back, or your hip. Your hot flashes come to an end; things droop. Spots appear. Your cleavage looks like a peach pit. If your elbows faced forward, you would kill yourself. You're two inches shorter than you used to be. You're ten pounds fatter and you cannot lose a pound of it to save your soul. Your hands don't work as well as they once did and you can't open bottles, jars, wrappers, and especially those gadgets that are encased tightly in what seems to be molded Mylar. If you were stranded on a desert island and your food were sealed in plastic packaging, you would starve to death. You take so many pills in the morning you don't have room for breakfast.

Meanwhile, there is a new conversation, about CAT scans and MRIs. Everywhere you look there's cancer. Once a week there's some sort of bad news. Once a month there's a funeral. You lose close friends and discover one of the worst truths of old age: they're irreplaceable. People who run four miles a day and eat only nuts and berries drop dead. People who drink a quart of whiskey and smoke two packs of cigarettes a day drop dead. You are suddenly in a lottery, the ultimate game of chance, and someday your luck will run out. Everybody dies.

There's nothing you can do about it. Whether or not you eat six almonds a day. Whether or not you believe in God.

(Although there's no question a belief in God would come in handy. It would be great to think there's a plan, and that everything happens for a reason. I don't happen to believe that. And every time one of my friends says to me, "Everything happens for a reason," I would like to smack her.)

At some point I will be not just old, older, or oldish—I will be really old. I will be actively impaired by age: something will make it impossible for me to read, or speak, or hear what's being said, or eat what I want, or walk around the block. My memory, which I can still make jokes about, will be so dim that I will have to pretend I know what's going on.

The realization that I may have only a few good years remaining has hit me with real force, and I have done a lot of thinking as a result. I would like to have come up with something profound, but I haven't. I try to figure out what I really want to do every day, I try to say to myself, If this is one of the last days of my life, am I doing exactly what I want to be doing? I aim low. My idea of a perfect day is a frozen custard at Shake Shack and a walk in the park. (Followed by a Lactaid.) My idea of a perfect night is a good play and dinner at Orso. (But no garlic, or I won't be able to sleep.) The other day I found a bakery that bakes my favorite childhood cake, and it was everything I remembered; it made my week. The other night we were coming up the FDR Drive and Manhattan was doing its fabulous, magical, twinkling thing, and all I could think was how lucky I've been to spend my adult life in New York City.

We used to go to our house on Long Island every summer. We would drive out with the kids the day they got out of school and we wouldn't come back until Labor Day. We were always there for the end of June, my favorite time of the year, when the sun doesn't set until nine-thirty at night and you feel as if you will live forever. On July Fourth, there were fire-works at the beach, and we would pack a picnic, dig a hole in the sand, build a fire, sing songs—in short, experience a night when we felt like a conventional American family (instead of the divorced, patched-together, psychoanalyzed, oh-so-modern family we were).

In mid-July, the geese would turn up. They would fly overhead in formation, their wings beating the air in a series of heart-stopping whooshes. I was elated by the sound. The geese were not yet flying south, mostly they were just moving from one pond to another, but that moment of realizing (from the mere sound of beating wings) that birds were overhead was one of the things that made the summers out there so magical.

In time, of course, the kids grew up and it was just me and Nick in the house on Long Island. The sound of geese became a different thing—the first sign that summer was not going to last forever, and soon another year would be over. Then, I'm sorry to say, they became a sign not just that summer would come to an end, but that so would everything else. As a result, I stopped liking the geese. In fact, I began to hate them. I especially began to hate their sound, which was not beating wings—how could I have ever thought it was?—but a lot of uneuphonious honks.

Now we don't go to Long Island in the summer and I don't hear the geese. Sometimes, instead, we go to Los Angeles, where there are hummingbirds, and I love to watch them because they're so busy getting the most out of life.

What I Won't Miss

Dry skin
Bad dinners like the one we went to last night
E-mail
Technology in general
My closet
Washing my hair
Bras
Funerals
Illness everywhere
Polls that show that 32 percent of the
    American people believe in creationism

143

Polls
Fox
The collapse of the dollar
Joe Lieberman
Clarence Thomas
Bar mitzvahs
Mammograms
Dead flowers
The sound of the vacuum cleaner
Bills
E-mail. I know I already said it, but I want to
　emphasize it.
Small print
Panels on Women in Film
Taking off makeup every night

What I Will Miss

My kids
Nick
Spring
Fall
Waffles
The concept of waffles
Bacon
A walk in the park
The idea of a walk in the park
The park

Shakespeare in the Park
The bed
Reading in bed
Fireworks
Laughs
The view out the window
Twinkle lights
Butter
Dinner at home just the two of us
Dinner with friends
Dinner with friends in cities where none of us
   lives
Paris
Next year in Istanbul
Pride and Prejudice
The Christmas tree
Thanksgiving dinner
One for the table
The dogwood
Taking a bath
Coming over the bridge to Manhattan
Pie

Acknowledgments

I thank, as always, Delia Ephron, Bob Gottlieb, Amanda Urban, and Nick Pileggi.

And also Arianna Huffington, David Shipley, Shelley Wanger, David Remnick, Paul Bogaards, and Maria Verel.

And also J. J. Sacha.

And also, of course, my doctors.

A NOTE ABOUT THE AUTHOR

Nora Ephron is the author of the huge best seller **I Feel Bad About My Neck,** as well as **Heartburn, Crazy Salad, Wallflower at the Orgy,** and **Scribble Scribble.** She recently wrote and directed the hit movie **Julie & Julia** and has received Academy Award nominations for best original screenplay for **When Harry Met Sally . . . , Silkwood,** and **Sleepless in Seattle,** which she also directed. Her other credits include the current stage hit **Love, Loss, and What I Wore,** written with Delia Ephron. She lives in New York City with her husband, writer Nicholas Pileggi.